DATE DUE

PRESERVED FLOWERS

PRESSED & DRIED

PRESERVED FLOWERS

PRESSED & DRIED

DIANE FLOWERS

Sterling Publishing Co., Inc.
New York

Prolific Impressions Production Staff:
Editor in Chief: Mickey Baskett
Copy Editor: Phyllis Mueller
Graphics: Karen Turpin
Styling: Lenos Key
Photography: Jerry Mucklow
Administration: Jim Baskett

Every effort has been made to insure that the information presented is accurate. Since we have no control over physical conditions, individual skills, or chosen tools and products, the publisher disclaims any liability for injuries, losses, untoward results, or any other damages which may result from the use of the information in this book. Thoroughly read the instructions for all products used to complete the projects in this book, paying particular attention to all cautions and warnings shown for that product to ensure their proper and safe use.

Library of Congress Cataloging-in-Publication Data Available

2 4 6 8 10 9 7 5 3 1

Published by Sterling Publishing Co., Inc.
387 Park Avenue South, New York, NY 10016
© 2006 by Prolific Impressions, Inc.
Distributed in Canada by Sterling Publishing
c/o Canadian Manda Group, 165 Dufferin Street,
Toronto, Ontario, Canada M6K 3H6
Distributed in the United Kingdom by GMC Distribution Services,
Castle Place, 166 High Street, Lewes, East Sussex, England BN7 1XU
Distributed in Australia by Capricorn Link (Australia) Pty. Ltd.
P.O. Box 704, Windsor, NSW 2756, Australia

Printed in China

Sterling ISBN-13: 978-1-4027-2449-7
ISBN-10: 1-4027-2449-7

For information about custom editions, special sales, premium and corporate purchases, please contact Sterling Special Sales Department at 800-805-5489 or specialsales@sterlingpub.com.

ABOUT THE AUTHOR

DIANE FLOWERS

Diane Flowers is a self-taught creative designer and author. She opened her business in 1998, manufacturing, designing, and selling her own lines of home decorating accessories. In 2001, she joined the Society of Creative Designers and began selling her designs to manufacturers, editors, and book publishers.

Her love of working with all types of artificial, dried, and pressed flowers continues to inspire her to search for new and unique ways to combine flowers with a wide variety of other materials. Diane is the author of *Silk Flowers for Every Season* (2005). You can visit her website to see other examples of her work: www.MFTEnterprises.com.

THANK YOU

Many thanks to my family and friends and to the members of the Society of Creative Designers, for all of their encouragement and support, which allows me to pursue my passion of creating with flowers.

ACKNOWLEDGEMENTS

My personal thanks to the following companies that so generously provided their products for the projects in this book:

Dow Chemical Co. and Flora Craft, for Styrofoam® products.
Krylon, for spray sealers, adhesives, paints, and leafing pens.
Tombow, for acid free adhesive and metal glue.
Delta, for Sarah Lugg designer kits.
Nature's Pressed, for pressed flowers, leaves, glass coaster kits, and flower presses and designing tools.
DecoArt, for acrylic paints and mediums.
JanLynn, for papers.
Fiber Scraps, for antiquing paint.
Duncan, for crafting glue.
Crafter's Pick, for decoupage gel.

And special thanks to Beth Cecil, owner of Forever Flowers, for sharing her technique for making glass coasters, and Cinder and Glenn, owners of Meadows Direct, for sharing their technique for aging clay pots.

Styrofoam® is a registered trademark of the Dow Chemical Company.

CONTENTS

INTRODUCTION

Experiencing the joy of working with dried and pressed flowers and natural materials can be as simple as placing a jar of seasonal branches on your dining table to bring a little of the outdoors inside. This simple act can encourage you to look around your yard or garden, and observe what's growing at the sides of the road. You may discover that the colors and beauty of the natural world can inspire you with different wonders every month. As the seasons change, flowers and leaves offer endless potential for design inspiration and ideas.

This book shows you how to enjoy the call of the great outdoors and enrich your life indoors by preserving plant materials that can be used for arrangements, decorations, and gifts. You'll discover how simple it can be to build yourself a supply of dried plant materials using easy techniques for drying and pressing all kinds of flowers and foliage, and how to use those materials to create centerpieces, wreaths, swags, and wall and tabletop designs. (Of course, you can also buy all kinds of dried and pressed materials and use them to create the projects, and purchasing materials is a good way to augment your harvest or acquire items for your designs that don't grow in your area.)

Dried and pressed flower designs begin with an idea, a container or base form, and a few tools. When those three things are combined with beautiful dried and pressed blooms and foliage the result is an elegant, long-lasting creation that can enhance any room in your home. The projects in this book illustrate a variety of uses for dried and pressed flowers, leaves, and other types of foliage. You will see silica- and air-dried roses, hydrangea, sunflowers, bay leaves, rosemary and chilies. There are ideas for wreaths, picture frames, greeting cards, glass coasters, photo albums, and a scrapbook page, along with holiday ornaments and table and chair decorating ideas.

Once you understand some basic elements of designing with flowers you can experiment and develop your own unique style. Always remember that floral design is a subjective art; there is no right or wrong way to approach designing. Use these concepts and projects as starting points for creating both dried and pressed designs. And have some fun.

Don't be afraid to use your imagination to grow, harvest, and preserve your own materials. You don't need a field full of flowers – three or four plants of each type will yield enough stems for several designs. To grow them, just follow the directions on the seed packets, or consult reference books or gardening authorities in your area for guidance. I've included a list of common flowers and foliage and recommended methods for drying and preserving them to get you started.

Be aware that the process of drying and pressing flowers can be addictive – you'll find yourself wanting to try new techniques or improve upon your past results. After a few seasons of creating your own displays with flowers from your own garden you will soon understand why dried and pressed flowers are often called "everlastings." Though most of your preserved blooms won't last forever, the joy and pleasure of the experience of creating is everlasting.

TOOLS & SUPPLIES

Before you start preserving flowers and foliage for your arrangements and projects, you will need to gather some helpful tools and supplies. They are available at most craft supply stores, and you probably already have some of them in your home. You'll find detailed instructions for drying and pressing flowers and greenery in the following section, "Preserving Techniques."

Drying & Preserving Supplies

These are the tools and supplies you need to dry and preserve flowers and greenery. The "Preserving Techniques" section will give more information for using the supplies.

SILICA GEL:

This comes in crystals or powder. You can find this at most craft stores or craft departments. Many nurseries also carry this. It is used to cover flowers and foliage for drying. The flowers are layered in a container with silica gel between each layer. The crystals or powder are usually blue in color when they are ready to use; they turn pink when they absorb moisture. Silica can also be used to dry flowers and foliage in a microwave oven. You can reuse silica gel indefinitely by drying it in a low heat conventional oven or heating it in a microwave oven. Follow the manufacturer's instructions on the container.

GLYCERINE:

Mix this liquid with hot water to preserve foliage and some flowers. Stems are placed in the solution to soak up the glycerine. This process can take a week or more. When foliage or flowers are dried using this method, they remain relatively flexible but turn a darker color. Glycerine can be re-used if you add a drop of chlorine bleach to keep it fresh. Glycerine can be found in drug stores and supermarkets.

HOLDERS AND CONTAINERS:

For air drying, you can use buckets or cans to dry stems upright. For hang-drying, you can use racks, suspended wire or coat hangers. For flat-drying, you can use racks, flat screens, hardware cloth, or chicken wire.

For silica drying, you can use plastic or glass containers – but use only microwave-safe containers in a microwave oven. I like to use medium-size disposable plastic drinking cups for silica drying individual roses or other flowers, but do **not** use the cups in the microwave.

For glycerine drying, you can use glass pitchers, jars, or vases.

MICROWAVE OVEN:

You can use your microwave and microwave-safe containers to dry flowers and foliage with silica gel. Use mitts or insulated gloves for protection when handling heated containers.

SPRAY SEALERS:

Once your flowers are dried, use sealers to prevent dried materials from shattering and reabsorbing moisture. Although some dried materials do not require sealing, all delicate flowers

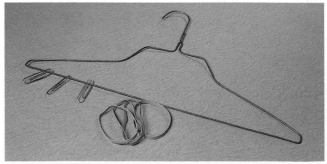

Wire hanger, paper clips, and rubber bands for hang drying.

Pictured clockwise from top left: Glass vase for air drying flowers, silica gel, glass casserole dish for microwaving, plastic container used for silica gel, glycerine, scoop for silica gel, soft bristle brush, measuring cup for glycerine, spray sealer

and silica-dried materials should be protected by spraying with a sealer. To protect yourself from fumes, do your spraying outdoors. *Always* read the labels and follow the manufacturer's instructions.

STORAGE BOXES:

Use various sizes of **cardboard boxes** with small holes for ventilation to store dried stems. Put heavier ones on the bottom.

OTHER TOOLS:

Soft bristle brush to brush away silica gel from flowers.

Rubber bands, for holding flower bunches together for air and hang drying. They will hold the stems securely in place as they dry and shrink.

Wire coat hangers (or fencing wire) and **paper clips**, for suspending bundled stems for air drying.

Flower Arranging Supplies

Having the proper tools and supplies makes arranging your flowers easy and fun. Craft stores and floral supply shops are good sources for floral arranging supplies.

WOODEN FLORAL PICKS:
These are used to hold or secure the stems in plastic foam for the arrangement. The picks are pointed at one end and have a thin wire attached to the other.

FLORAL PINS:
These are also called greening pins. They are U-shaped wires with sharp ends for securing stems, moss, or any accessory to plastic foam.

FLORAL TAPE:
This tape stretches and is available in various shades of green and brown. It wraps and binds wires and stems together. Floral tape is not an adhesive tape, but because it has a wax coating, it clings to itself when stretched.

FLORAL WIRE:
This wire comes in different lengths, colors, and gauges. I like to use 21 gauge green coated wire on spools or paddles. You can also buy floral wire precut (22 gauge works well) in different lengths and trim it yourself with wire cutters. I like to use brown bark-covered wire to create natural looking hangers.

SKEWERS:
Thin wooden or bamboo skewers are a versatile tool I like to keep around. They can be used to lengthen stems, to attach fruit in arrangements, or to make holes in floral foam for inserting stems.

CUTTING TOOLS:
You will need a good pair of **hand shears or clippers** to cut dried flower stems. For thicker stems, use **pruning shears**. Use **household or sewing scissors** to cut ribbons and a **paper trimmer** tool to cut paper when a straight edge is desired.

A **serrated knife** is best for cutting and trimming foam. TIP: Rub the knife edge across a candle or bar of soap before cutting the foam.

Use medium size **wire cutters** when cutting wires to avoid straining your hands.

CONTAINERS:
When selecting a container or base, consider the size, shape, color, and texture of the overall design and the setting in which the arrangement will be displayed. **Baskets, jars, trays, pots, and vases**, in metal, clay, tin, ceramic, and wood are only a few of the types of containers available.

BASES:
Plastic foam (such as Styrofoam® brand foam), is available in shapes such as wreaths, cones, blocks, and balls. It is hard, porous, and inflexible and should be used with sturdier stems and for adding height and shape to designs. It works well for filling containers because it can be easily cut and shaped.

Wire forms and shapes can also be used as bases for dried flower designs such as wreaths.

Dry Floral foam is a common base material for holding dried stems and other materials. It can be used with or without a container. It is a softer foam, but crumbles easily. When working with dried flowers, use a type of foam specifically for use with dried flowers – it works much better. It is finely textured, brown or green in color, and may be labeled "dry foam."

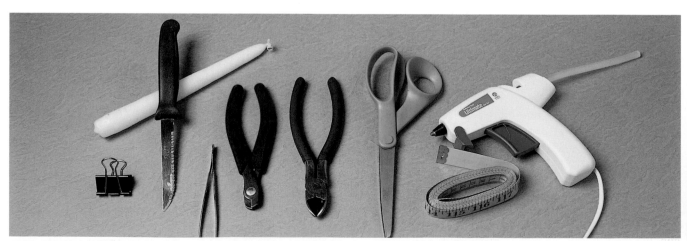

Flower Arranging Tools, pictured left to right: Binder clip for holding, knife and wax candle for cutting foam, tweezers, stem cutters, wire cutters, scissors, measuring tape, glue gun.

1) Foam shapes, 2) Spray adhesive, 3) Bark-covered wire, 4) Floral adhesive, 5) Skewers, 6) Stem wire, 7) Floral tape, 8) Floral pins,
9) Paddle wire, 10) Wire, 11) Wooden picks, 12) Moss

ADHESIVES:

Floral adhesive tape also known as anchor tape, and **floral clay**, which has a putty-like consistency, are used to secure foam blocks and pieces inside containers.

Hot glue works perfectly for attaching flowers to wires and stems, gluing accessories on wreaths, repairing shattered blooms, and securing floral foam in containers, among other uses. It dries quickly and holds extremely well. Glue guns come in a variety of sizes and temperatures. I prefer a low-temp glue gun, but any type will work for dried flower designing.

Use **spray adhesive**, for quickly adhering materials to foam or other bases or surfaces. CAUTION: Most sprays have toxic fumes and should be used outdoors or in well-ventilated areas.

MOSS:

Moss is used to cover foam and other base materials. The most common mosses are sheet moss, reindeer moss, and Spanish moss. I like to use green reindeer moss to cover foam bases and as an accent in designs and natural reindeer moss with clay pots and seashells. I also use moss to cover exposed spots of hot glue.

Flower Pressing & Project Making Supplies

Pressed flowers are wonderful embellishments for cards, gift tags, scrapbook pages, coasters, and holiday ornaments. They also look lovely displayed in frames. You can purchase pressed flowers in the floral departments of crafts stores, but it's easy to make your own. Use **shoe boxes or hat boxes** for storing pressed materials. Keep them in separate manila or glassine envelopes or between pieces of tissue or blotting paper.

FLOWER PRESS:

This can be purchased at most craft shops or departments, nurseries, and many gift shop. It contains everything you need to press flowers and leaves. Usually it contains layers of cardboard and absorbent paper with a wooden top and bottom that can be tightened with the bolts and nuts that are attached to it. You can also **make your own** flower press with two pieces of wood, some papers and cardboard, and four bolts with wing nuts.

TWEEZERS:

You will need tweezers to position pressed flowers and leaves. Pressed materials are very fragile and can break if you handle them with your fingers.

FRAMES AND GLASS SHAPES:

All sizes and styles of picture frames can be used to frame pressed designs, and you can embellish frames by adding pressed flowers and leaves. Glass squares, ovals, and other shapes provide an excellent base for displaying and preserving pressed materials. Use **adhesive-backed metal tape**, which comes in a variety of colors, to wrap glass pieces to protect, seal, and cover the cut glass edges.

DECORATIVE PAPERS:

Scrapbooking and other decorative and handmade papers provide excellent backgrounds for pressed flower and leaf designs. Layer papers to add texture and dimension.

EMBELLISHMENTS:

Buttons, beads, twine, ribbon, seashells, candles, and raffia are just a few of the embellishments you can use to add interest and depth to your pressed displays. TIP: Try to incorporate things that have special meaning to you (or to the recipient, if you're making a gift), such as travel souvenirs, into your designs.

ADHESIVES

Any white **craft glue** works well for securing pressed flowers and leaves. Use very small amounts if you want a natural look or if you will be covering your pressed design with glass. If you prefer a flat appearance and want to cover the pressed materials with decoupage medium, use a water-and-glue mixture to secure the flowers and leaves. Apply the water-and-glue mix with a paint brush, completely covering the backs of the pressed materials before positioning them on surfaces.

Decoupage medium, which comes in liquid and gel forms, is a good method for adhering, sealing, and protecting pressed materials.

Specialty glues, such as metal glue, paper and acid-free glue, glue dots, and acid-free adhesive-backed tape are handy for particular circumstances. You'll find recommended adhesives for each project in the "Supplies" lists of the individual project instructions.

Adhesives, pictured left to right, back row: Disposable bowl for mixing water and glue, paper/acid-free glue, white craft glue, metal glue, decoupage gel, clear gel craft glue. Front row: Adhesive-backed tape, glue dots

Flower Pressing Supplies, pictured clockwise from top center: paper towels, iron, waxed paper, cardboard sheets and rubber bands, wooden flower press.

YOUR WORK AREA:

You will need to create a comfortable work area. Choose a place with good lighting, a work table at a comfortable height, and lots of space so you can spread out your materials. When working with pressed materials, you need a clean, smooth work surface such as brown kraft paper, freezer paper, or poster board. Since hot glue drippings and scratches from stem cutters and wires are common occurrences, you may want to use a piece of plywood to protect your table top.

Most flower arranging is done standing, but you can sit on a stool as long as your work table is at a comfortable height.

If you want to create wreaths or other types of wall designs, having a place to hang the wreath or base form as you work will allow you to properly secure your materials and give you the correct visual perspective for good placement and balance.

PRESERVING TECHNIQUES

This section outlines several methods of drying and preserving flowers and foliage:

- Pressing
- Air and water drying
- Drying with glycerine
- Drying with silica gel
- Microwave drying.

There is a list at the end of this section of recommendations for drying specific types of plants.

Drying flowers is not an exact process, and some materials work better than others. Many materials have been used to preserve flowers, including sawdust, washing powder, talcum powder, alcohol, cornstarch, cornmeal, borax, sand, antifreeze, and even kitty litter. No one method or material is considered best because what works well for one flower may not work at all for another – even flowers from the same plant may not turn out the same. You'll need to experiment to determine which methods work best in the type of climate where you live and for the types of flowers and leaves you have.

Skill also plays a part – a person skilled in a certain technique may get good results, while another person may get poor results using the same technique and the same type of flowers.

Whichever method you choose to use, the principle of drying is to remove moisture slowly while maintaining as much of the original shape and texture as possible. Drying is complete when flowers or leaves are crisp and dry to the touch but not brittle. The thickest parts are the slowest to dry.

Harvesting

There is no one particular time of the year to collect materials for drying or pressing. It's a good idea, however, to decide what plant materials you will dry and preserve and the methods you will use before you begin cutting and pruning. Almost any plant part (flowers, leaves, stems) can be dried or pressed.

You will want to harvest your flowers just as the blooms reach maturity. In the summer, that means checking your garden daily – a bloom that's closed one day could be fully open the next. The best time of day to cut is midmorning, after the dew has dried but before the flowers have wilted from the afternoon heat because dampness will cause mold and mildew. If you live in a rainy area, your main concern will be to harvest when the plants are dry, even if it means you'll have to cut them early in the morning.

Pick materials that are in prime condition. Petals with brown spots or bug-eaten edges only look worse after drying. It's a good idea to harvest more flowers than you think you will need. You will probably lose a few in the process of drying, pressing and, storing.

Wildflowers, many of which are protected, can usually be cut in small numbers wherever you find them, but it's more appropriate to buy a package of flowers seeds and grow them yourself. This is an easy solution if you want to pick a lot of them for use indoors or want to preserve them in quantity.

Use a bucket of water to hold freshly cut stems intended for silica drying and a basket to hold stems for air-drying. If you plan to air dry, leave as much stem on your cutting as possible – you'll need the extra length for hanging and for height in your designs. Keep stems for air-drying as fresh as possible before you hang them or place them on racks – don't let them wilt. Position flowers you plan to press in your flower press immediately after cutting.

Besides flowers, there are other wonderful materials that can be found in your own garden or backyard. If you prune in autumn and spring, you will have a bounty of materials to use for seasonal designs, pressing, and drying. Twigs, leaves, nuts, and cones are only a few of the things you can find on the ground without having to cut anything. Trips to the beach are a wonderful source for shells and other unusual items. In winter, collect twigs and leaves.

Color Changes

When dry, flower colors will appear several shades darker. Red flowers may turn purple, brown, or almost black. Creamy white flowers may turn darker, pale yellow, or brown. Blue, purple, lavender, yellow, and orange flowers, when dry, are more likely to keep their original colors.

When pressed, brighter colors will tend to dry more true to color while the darker colors such as red and purple may darken slightly. Light pastel colors may slightly fade. Leaves retain most of their original color when pressed.

PRESSING

Most flowers and leaves are suitable for pressing except those with bulky centers or thick, fleshy leaves. You will need to make a judgment about the flowers you wish to press to make sure this method is the most effective for them. Flat flowers that don't have bulky centers such as pansies or violets press best. You can take some flowers apart to press, such as hydrangeas where you would press each individual flower section. Roses won't press well, but individual petals press beautifully.

Purchase a flower press or make your own using plywood, blotting paper, plain cardboard, bolts and wing nuts. If your purchased flower kit comes with corrugated cardboard, I suggest you replace it with plain cardboard as the corrugated design could leave ridges across your flower petals.

The Basic Process:
1. Place a piece of plain cardboard in the bottom of the press. (**Photo 1**)
2. Add a layer of blotting paper. (**Photo 2**)
3. Position the flowers or leaves on the blotting paper so they do not touch each other. (**Photo 3**)
4. Cover the leaves or flowers with blotting paper and cardboard. (**Photo 4**) Stack layers of paper, flowers, and cardboard in the press until you've used all your materials or the press is full.
5. Place the top of your press on the stack and secure the bolts and wing nuts. (**Photo 5**)
6. After a few days tighten the bolts again – as the flowers dry, they will shrink. Flowers can take between one and three weeks to dry; leaves usually take one week.

Optional Method: Place flowers between the pages of a phone book or sheets of newsprint and put weights on top. When pressing in a book or between newspaper, place facial tissues on the pages to aid in moisture absorption. Check the flowers at the end of a week. Change the facial tissue if it seems damp and the flowers are not yet dry.

Pressing Tips:
• Flowers should be in their prime condition for pressing – no insect holes.
• For a variety of design possibilities, press flowers that are in different stages of development, from buds up to full maturity. This will give you a variety of sizes and usually color variations to work with when designing a project.
• Pick your flowers when the weather is dry.
• For even pressing, place flowers of the same thickness together in layers.

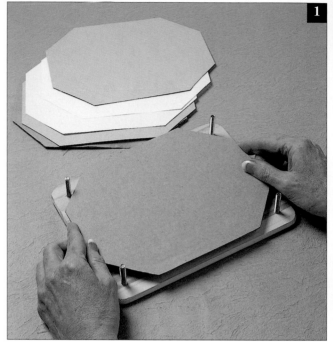

Photo 1 – Placing the cardboard.

• Cut odd-shaped flowers or buds in half and open them for pressing.
• Press individual petals and assemble them after pressing to make flowers.

Microwave Pressing:
Another quick pressing method can be done in a microwave oven. You'll need to experiment to find the best setting and timing for your microwave. Start with the lowest power setting.
1. Cut two 10" squares of cardboard.
2. Place two paper towels and four facial tissues on one piece of cardboard.
3. Position the flowers on the tissues, being sure they do not touch.
4. Place four more tissues and two more paper towels on top of the flowers.
5. Cover them with the other piece of cardboard and secure them with rubber bands.
6. Place them in a microwave oven. For leaves and thin flowers, heat for 1-1/2 minutes. Allow to cool for 10 minutes and check the dryness. (The cardboard, tissues, and towels will become wet and will need to be replaced.) Repeat the process until the plant materials are dry.

Photo 2 – Placing the blotting paper.

Photo 3 – Positioning the plant material for drying.

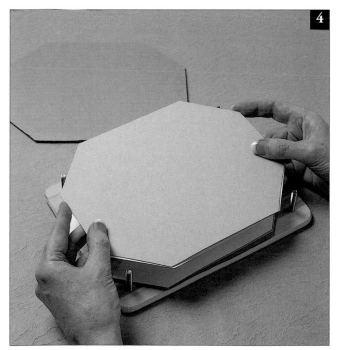

Photo 4 – Adding a layer of blotting paper.

Photo 5 – Securing the top of the press.

HEAT PRESSING

I'm sure we all remember picking leaves in the fall, bringing them in and letting our mothers help us press them between sheets of waxed paper. This is a wonderful way to preserve colorful leaves and other flat plant material.

You will need sheets of waxed paper and an iron. Place a piece of cardboard down on your ironing board. Place a sheet of waxed paper on top of the cardboard. Arrange leaves or other material on waxed paper. Do not allow plant material to touch. Place another piece of waxed paper on top of plant material. Press with hot DRY iron. Let the plant materials cool completely before handling. Peel from waxed paper and discard paper.

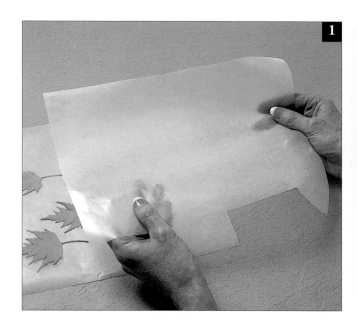

Photo 1 – Place the plant material on a sheet of wax paper. Cover with another sheet of wax paper.

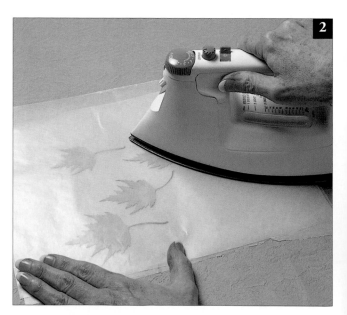

Photo 2 – Press with a medium hot dry iron until flat and dry. Replace the wax paper with each pressing.

AIR DRYING

The easiest, most common, and least expensive method of drying flowers is air drying. Air drying techniques include **hang drying** (hanging flower bundles upside down), **upright drying** (standing plant materials upright in empty buckets), and **Rack drying** (placing foliage or flower heads flat on drying racks). You can also arrange freshly cut stems while they are still soft and flexible and allow them to dry naturally. If you like a lot of dimension in your designs, air drying will allow your stems to assume their natural, gently curving forms.

Air drying usually takes between three days and three weeks. The amount of time varies with fluctuations in air temperature and humidity and differs according to stem thickness, bundle size, and plant species. For best results choose a location that is dark, warm, and dry with good ventilation. Some possible locations might be a large closet, a spare bedroom, or a storage building.

HANG DRYING
Hang drying is the easiest method. You can use suspended wires or coat hangers and paper clips to suspend your bunches, making sure they hang perpendicular to the ground and are far enough apart to allow good air circulation.

UPRIGHT DRYING
Flowers with large heads can be difficult to hang dry – gravity can distort them while they are hanging upside down. For some flowers, upright drying in containers is the solution. Upright drying does not require a lot of space and the effects of gravity sometimes create interesting arched shapes.

ADDING WIRE STEMS BEFORE DRYING
You can insert stem wire in the flower head before drying, if you prefer. Simply trim the stem to about 1/4", insert the wire into the stem, and dry the flowers upright in a container. As the stem dries around the wire it will form a tight bond. For extra security before use, add a small amount of hot glue where the stem and wire meet. Wrap the wire stem with floral tape.

RACK DRYING
Another air drying option is rack drying. You can make a rack for drying by attaching chicken wire, hardware cloth, or window screen to a wood or metal frame. (You could also simply use a window screen from a hardware store.) If you use chicken wire or hardware cloth, you can dry the flowers upright with the stems attached by inserting the stems of the flowers through the wire. Or trim the stems and position the flower heads on the screen.

Photo 1 – Gather several of the same type of stems together. Secure them with a rubber band.

Photo 2 – Hang the bunch upside down to dry. Here, I've used paper clips to attach the bundles to a wire coat hanger.

Photo 3 – Water drying roses.

WATER DRYING
Water drying preserves the flowers' original shape better than air drying, but it takes much longer.
1. Place the stems in cold water inside a container so they do not touch.
2. Place the container in a dark, dry, well ventilated area. As the water evaporates the flowers will dry out. They should be completely dry in three to four weeks.

21

Photo 1 – Pouring silica gel crystals in a container.

Photo 2 – Placing a flower in the silica gel.

Photo 3 – Gently pouring silica gel crystals over the flower.

Photo 4 – Covering the container.

SILICA GEL DRYING

You can dry almost any flower with silica gel. The most suitable ones are those with fairly simple flowers because more complex flowers make it difficult to get the silica between the petals, resulting in uneven drying. If you are uncertain about which drying method to use, silica gel will usually produce the best results for most materials.

The Basic Process:

1. Pour a 1" layer of silica gel crystals into a shallow, airtight plastic or glass container. (**Photo 1**)

2. Position the flowers in the container. (**Photo 2**) How you do this depends on the type of flower. *If the flowers have multiple layers of petals,* place them face up on top of the crystals, positioning the blooms so they do not overlap or touch the sides of the container. *If the flowers have a single layer of petals or very dense centers,* place them face down.

3. Use a spoon or small scoop to gently pour more crystals over the flowers, covering them completely. Be careful to not compress the petals. (**Photo 3**) *Option: Mound silica gel around the flowers against the sides of the container, then gently tap the container to distribute the silica gel over the flower until the bloom is completely covered. Gently tapping the container will even out the crystals without crushing the petals.*

4. Secure the lid on the container (**Photo 4**) and allow to dry for two to seven days. Larger flowers can take ten days or longer – the length of time will vary depending on the type and thickness of the plant material.

5. After two days, slowly pour off the top layer of crystals into another container and check the blooms for crispness. Grasp the stem to lift the flower from the silica gel. (**Photo 5**) If they are not dry, pour the silica back over them, replace the lid, and wait another day or two before checking them again. Try not to leave them in the silica longer than necessary.

6. Dried blooms are extremely fragile! After your flowers are dry, carefully remove any residue with a soft brush, holding them by the stems. (**Photo 6**)

Two options for Drying Thicker Stems:

Option 1. If the flower base around the stem takes longer than the outside petals to dry completely, remove the gel from the thinner, outside petals that are already dry and leave the base and stem covered until dry. Be sure to check them the next day.

Option 2. Another way to finish drying thicker stems is to remove the flowers from the silica and let the stems air dry.

Reusing Silica Gel:

Silica gel can be reused and rejuvenated by pouring it into an uncovered glass container and placing it in a 275-degree oven for about an hour. The blue color will return when the crystals are dry and ready to be reused.

You can also place a small amount of crystals in a microwave-safe dish and heat them on high for five minutes, stirring every minute, until the blue crystals reappear.

Allow the rejuvenated crystals to return to room temperature before covering more blooms. Store the cooled crystals in airtight containers.

Other Desiccants for Drying:

Instead of silica gel, you can also use borax, cornmeal, fine sand, or cat litter as desiccants for drying. (Because of its coarse texture, cat litter is not recommended for delicate flowers.) Some people like a mixture of sand and borax or borax and cornmeal. Use the same process described for silica gel drying.

Photo 5 – Lifting the dried flower by its stem.

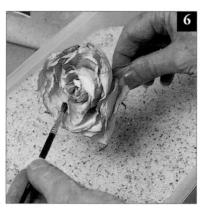

Photo 6 – Using a brush to carefully remove any particles of silica gel.

Drying large flower heads: Large flowers, such as sunflowers, take a long time to dry – up to ten days – even with silica, and they require special handling. For good results, use a box as a container. Keep about 24 inches of stem attached to the flower and cover the flower heads with silica, allowing the stems to hang over the sides of the container. Wrap and seal with plastic kitchen wrap and wait at least one week.

Drying small blooms: When silica drying roses or smaller blooms, I place each bloom in a separate disposable plastic drinking cup. The cups are deeper than many containers and use less silica gel. I cover the cups with kitchen plastic wrap and check them after two days.

MICROWAVE DRYING

You can also silica dry flowers in a microwave oven, and the drying time can be significantly reduced. Actual drying times vary, depending on the type of flower and the power of the oven. See the box, "Microwave Drying Times." Experiment to determine the best drying times and settings for your own microwave.

Microwave drying tends to alter flower color more dramatically than the conventional silica drying method. Light pink flowers may turn pale yellow; more vibrant colors retain their colors best. Flowers with very thick petals or flowers with very thin petals do not dry well in the microwave and fully opened flowers may lose their petals after microwave drying.

The technique is the same as silica gel drying, but only dry a few flowers at one time.

The Basic Process:

1. Place a layer of silica gel crystals or powder in a microwave-safe container, such as a glass bowl. Place the flower on the silica gel. (**Photo 1**)

2. Gently pour more silica gel over the bloom to cover it completely. (**Photo 2**) If you pour too quickly, the petals could bend or be crushed.

3. Place the container, uncovered, in the microwave.

4. Heat at medium power for one minute.

5. Allow plant material to cool to room temperature. (This takes 15 to 30 minutes.)

6. When cool, remove the silica gel and check for dryness. If the blooms are not dry, re-cover them and repeat the process.

Microwave Drying Times:

When using the microwave with silica gel, **always** experiment before drying a large number of flowers or leaves. Based on my experience, here are some recommendations:

• Roses and large orchids – up to 2-1/2 minutes

• Daisies, zinnias, marigolds, carnations, mums, and small orchids – 1-1/2 minutes

• Large dahlias, peonies, and mums – 3 minutes.

• Leaves and foliage – 1 minute

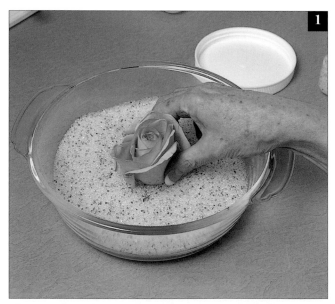

Photo 1 – Place flower in silica gel.

Photo 2 – Cover with more silica gel.

DRYING WITH GLYCERINE

This method works well with most foliage and evergreens. And it works better with foliage than with flowers. Leaves usually will turn brown, but different types of plants turn different shades of straw colors, to olive, to tan, to nearly black, and they remain flexible. Experimentation is required to know the exact effect. Glycerine can be found in drug stores and supermarkets.

Usually the best time to preserve foliage is during the growing season – June to September. Some evergreens can be preserved all year round. Cut a stem of foliage, cutting the end at an angle, then make a cross cut. Make sure the stem is no longer than about 12". Remove any damaged leaves. Because glyccrine is thicker than water, you will want to make sure that the stems will soak up the glycerine and not get clogged. To get your stems prepared, place the stem ends in warm water for at least a few hours, or overnight.

The Basic Process:

1. Mix two parts very hot water with one part glycerine.
2. Trim the ends of the stems and make a cross cut in the end of each one. (**Photo 1**)

3. Place the plant material in a vase or jar and pour 3" of the glycerine mixture into the container. (**Photo 2**)
4. Store the container in a warm, dark, dry place for about three weeks (or as long as it takes to preserve the foliage. Check the stems daily – you will see the solution as it is taken up into the stems and veins of the leaves. Add more of the glycerine mixture if it starts to evaporate. When the solution reaches the top of the leaf, the plant is done. Do not allow the plant material to stay in the solution too long – that can cause bleeding (where the glycerine comes out through the leaves) or molding and is very messy.
5. Remove the stems. Trim the parts that were submerged in the glycerine mixture.
6. Bundle the stems together with a rubber band and hang them upside down to dry in a warm, dark location for about two weeks or use them immediately.

NOTE: The glycerine mixture can be reused, even if it has turned brown. Strain it through a sieve to remove any plant material or debris and add a drop of chlorine bleach to keep it fresh.

Photo 1 – Cutting the stems.

Photo 2 – The plant material in the container.

STORAGE

Regardless of how you choose to dry or press your flowers and other materials, be sure to store them carefully if you will not be using them immediately. They are fragile and will last longer if they are kept in a dry, dark, and cool environment.

Store **dried flowers** in covered boxes that will allow air to circulate. Cardboard boxes work well if you make some holes in the sides and top. Keep the boxes in a place that's not too damp (i.e., your basement) or too dry (your attic). If you live in a humid climate, it's a good idea to store silica-dried flowers in airtight plastic containers with a small amount of silica gel inside. Temperature is not as important as humidity; cool areas (like an unheated garage) are generally better.

Store glycerine and air-dried flowers the same way as silica dried flowers, but do not store them in the same boxes. Moisture in glycerine-treated flowers can damage air- and silica-dried flowers.

Storing Dried Flowers:

1. Seal your dried flowers with a spray sealer to coat and strengthen the brittle stems and blooms and to keep the flowers from re-absorbing moisture from the air. Allow the sealer to dry completely.
2. After they are dry, wrap each bunch loosely in tissue paper or newsprint.
3. Lay the bunches flat in a storage box.

- Put heavy flowers on the bottom and more delicate flowers on top of them.
- Do not pack the box too tightly.

4. Label your boxes and keep them in the same cool dry areas that you used to dry your flowers.

Storing Pressed Flowers:

Pressed flowers can be stored between layers of tissue paper or in envelopes inside shoeboxes or hat boxes.

Rejuvenating Dried Flowers:

- If your dried flowers do not hold their shape you can lightly steam them by holding them over boiling water, rearrange the petals, and allow them to air dry.
- Use a toothpick to apply tiny spots of hot glue to re-attach loose petals to the stems.

Deterring Pests:

The two common pests that destroy dried flowers are moths and mice. Moths can burrow deep into the blooms and cause the blooms to fall apart. You can kill the moth larvae by placing infected flowers in a plastic bag and putting them into a freezer for a few days. As a preventive measure, place some mothballs in your storage boxes.

To prevent damage from mice, you will need to set traps and store your flowers in thick plastic containers.

CARE

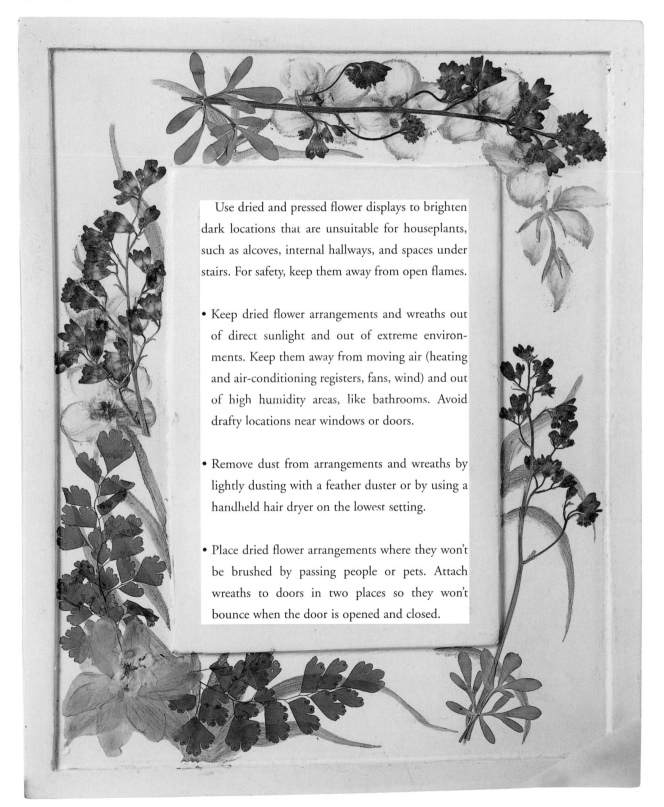

Use dried and pressed flower displays to brighten dark locations that are unsuitable for houseplants, such as alcoves, internal hallways, and spaces under stairs. For safety, keep them away from open flames.

• Keep dried flower arrangements and wreaths out of direct sunlight and out of extreme environments. Keep them away from moving air (heating and air-conditioning registers, fans, wind) and out of high humidity areas, like bathrooms. Avoid drafty locations near windows or doors.

• Remove dust from arrangements and wreaths by lightly dusting with a feather duster or by using a handheld hair dryer on the lowest setting.

• Place dried flower arrangements where they won't be brushed by passing people or pets. Attach wreaths to doors in two places so they won't bounce when the door is opened and closed.

DRYING METHOD RECOMMENDATIONS

Flowers that dry and press well are typically colorful, compact, strong-stemmed, and relatively low in moisture content. These lists include plants suitable for drying and the recommended techniques for each one. They are by no means exhaustive so you may not scc some plants you have previously dried successfully. When in doubt, experiment before you attempt to dry your most prized blooms.

Each plant will react differently depending upon when it was harvested, the drying method used, the individual species, temperature, and humidity level.

Colors will probably change. Pinks may lighten or darken, reds may become more purple, whites may darken. Blues, lavenders, yellows, and oranges may not change at all or they may become more intense.

Plants with fleshy leaves, such as succulents, are not suitable for drying. (They often just rot.) Most flowers, leaves, and foliage can be pressed.

LEAVES & FOLIAGE

- Aspen – Air or Silica Dry
- Bamboo – Air Dry or Glycerine
- Bay – Air or Silica Dry
- Birch – Air, Glycerine or Silica Dry
- Boxwood – Air, Glycerine or Silica Dry
- Camellia – Air, Glycerine or Silica Dry
- Cattail – Air Dry
- Cedar – Air Dry or Glycerine
- Dill – Air or Silica Dry
- Dogwood – Air or Silica Dry
- Dusty Miller – Air Dry
- Eucalyptus – Air, Glycerine or Silica Dry
- Fern – Air, Glycerine or Silica Dry
- Grasses (all types) – Air Dry or Glycerine
- Hawthorn – Air, Glycerine or Silica Dry
- Holly – Air, Glycerine or Silica Dry
- Honeysuckle – Air, Glycerine or Silica Dry
- Hosta – Air or Silica Dry
- Ivy – Air, Glycerine or Silica Dry
- Juniper – Air Dry or Glycerine
- Lamb's Ear – Air Dry
- Magnolia – Air Dry or Glycerine
- Maple – Air, Glycerine or Silica Dry
- Myrtle – Air, Glycerine or Silica Dry
- Oak – Air, Glycerine or Silica Dry
- Palm – Air Dry or Glycerine
- Rhododendron – Air, Glycerine or Silica Dry
- Rosemary – Air, Glycerine or Silica Dry
- Pussy Willow – Air Dry
- Sage – Air or Silica Dry
- Salal – Air, Glycerine or Silica Dry

FLOWERS

- Artichoke – Air or Silica Dry
- Azalea – Silica Dry
- Baby's Breath – Air or Silica Dry
- Bells of Ireland – Air or Silica Dry
- Black-eyed Susan – Air or Silica Dry
- Calla Lily – Silica Dry
- Camellia – Silica Dry
- Celosia – Air or Silica Dry
- Chinese Lantern – Air or Silica Dry
- Chrysanthemum – Air or Silica Dry
- Coneflowers – Air or Silica Dry
- Cosmos – Silica Dry
- Daffodil – Silica Dry
- Dahlia – Air or Silica Dry
- Daisy – Air or Silica Dry
- Delphinium – Silica Dry
- Dianthus – Air or Silica Dry
- Dogwood – Silica Dry
- Echinops – Air or Silica Dry
- Freesia – Silica Dry
- Foxglove – Air or Silica Dry
- Geranium – Silica Dry
- Gladiolus – Silica Dry
- Goldenrod – Air Dry
- Heather – Air or Silica Dry
- Hibiscus – Silica Dry
- Hollyhock – Air or Silica Dry
- Hops – Air Dry
- Hyacinth – Air or Silica Dry
- Hydrangea – Air or Silica Dry
- Iris – Silica Dry

- Larkspur – Air or Silica Dry
- Lavender – Air Dry
- Lilac – Silica Dry
- Lily – Silica Dry
- Marigold – Air or Silica Dry
- Nigella – Air or Silica Dry
- Orchid – Silica Dry
- Oregano – Air Dry
- Pansy – Silica Dry
- Peony – Air or Silica Dry
- Pepper – Air Dry
- Pitcher Plant – Air or Silica Dry
- Poppy – Air or Silica Dry
- Protea – Air or Silica Dry
- Queen Anne's Lace – Air or Silica Dry
- Rose – Air or Silica Dry
- Rosehips – Air or Silica Dry
- Rhododendron – Silica Dry
- Safflower – Air or Silica Dry
- Snapdragon – Silica Dry
- Statice – Air Dry
- Stock – Silica Dry
- Strawflower – Air or Silica Dry
- Sunflower – Air or Silica Dry
- Thistle – Air Dry
- Tulip – Silica Dry
- Verbena – Silica Dry
- Veronica – Air Dry
- Viola and Violets – Silica Dry
- Yarrow – Air Dry
- Zinnia – Silica Dry

BASIC TECHNIQUES

This section shows some of the basic techniques used when working with dried and pressed flowers to create arrangements or other decorative items. These techniques will save you time and help you create long-lasting arrangements. See the "Tools & Supplies" section for more information on the supplies needed.

Extending Stems

Photo 1 – Inserting a stem wire in a dried flower.

Photo 2 – Wrapping the stem wire with floral tape.

Adding Wire Stems with Tape:

Use stem wire and floral tape to extend the stems of dried flowers for arrangements. I like to use 12-inch, 21 gauge wire for stems. You can use this technique for attaching individual flowers or small bundles of flowers to wires.

1. Insert the stem in the wire. (**Photo 1**)
2. Grasp the end of the floral tape and the top of the wire where it meets the flower stem between your thumb and forefinger. (**Photo 2**) Roll the tape and wire between your fingers in one direction while gently stretching the tape downward with your other hand. As the tape winds in a spiral it will cover the wire.

Using Dried Stems & Wire with Tape:

You can trim the stems from your flowers, dry them separately, and reattach them or attach any other stems that you may have available to support your dried flowers. Use a small amount of hot glue to attach the end of the dried flower stem to a wire. Insert the wire in the flower. Wrap the wire with floral tape.

Attaching Picks:

Floral picks with wires can be used to lengthen stems and to secure stems and other accessories (like pine cones) to foam. The picks are short so this method is used when only a small length is needed to be added. I use this method most often when making wreaths where the plant materials are stuck into foam wreath bases.

1. To lengthen a stem, hold the pick and the stem together. Wrap the wire from the pick around the stem. To hide the wire, wrap the pick with floral tape. (**Photo 3**)

2. To attach a pick to a pine cone, wrap the wire attached to the pick around the pine cone until it is firmly attached. (**Photo 4**)

Attaching Clusters to a Pick:

This technique is used to add some length to delicate clusters of flowers so that they can be inserted into an arrangement or a wreath. This method can be used with a pick or a longer stem.

1. Cut a piece of heavier gauge wire than what comes on the pick. You won't be using the wire on the pick. Insert this small piece of wire through the center of the cluster. (**Photo 5**)

2. Bend the wire and bring the ends together. Twist the ends a few times. (**Photo 6**)

3. Place a floral pick beside the wire ends. Wrap the wires and the pick with floral tape. (**Photo 7**)

Photo 4 – Attaching pick to pine cone.

Photo 5 – Insert wire through flower cluster.

Photo 6 – Wrap ends of wire together under cluster.

Photo 7 – Cover wire with floral tape.

Photo 3 – Wrap pick wire around stem.

Photo 1 – Use hot glue to attach a piece of wire to a leaf when you need to extend the leaf stem length.

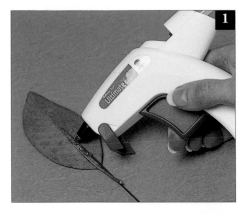

Photo 2 – Add the leaf stem to a flower cluster by wrapping with floral tape.

Photo 3 – Rub a serrated knife across an old candle or bar of soap before cutting foam to make the cutting easier.

Photo 4 – Use a knife to cut a foam block to fit into the container.

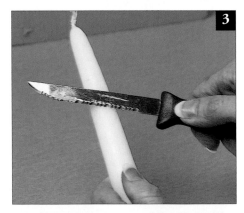

Adding Leaves to Wire Stems

It's easy to add individual leaves to stems of flowers. Extend the stem of the flower if needed, following previous instructions for "Extending Stems." You will need a hot glue gun and glue sticks.

1. Use hot glue to attach a wire stem to the back of a leaf (you may need to use a lot of glue). (**Photo 1**)

2. Wrap the stem of the leaf to the wire with floral tape. This adds extra security.

3. To add the leaf to a flower, place the wire stem with the leaf alongside the flower stem and wrap the two stems with floral tape. (**Photo 2**)

Adding Foam to Containers

I use foam as the base for most of my arrangements. For a secure arrangement, the foam should be cut to fit snugly in the container. Evaluate your design and container to determine if you need to trim the foam even with the container top or if you want to allow it to extend above the top to add height and shape to your design. Cut the foam to size with a serrated-edge knife. (**Photos 3 & 4**)

If the foam block is too small for the container, use hot glue to secure it to the bottom and insert smaller pieces around the sides to secure it. TIP: If you intend to remove the arrangement later, use small pieces of floral adhesive tape or floral clay instead of hot glue.

After you have placed the foam in the container, place 4 pieces of floral adhesive tape across the top of the foam in a criss-cross pattern, anchoring ends of tape to the sides of the container.

Securing Flowers in Foam

The stems of some dried flowers break when inserted in soft foam or may not stay securely inserted in the foam. To avoid this, make holes in the foam with a wooden skewer or wire stem before inserting the flowers. Use hot glue to secure them.

1. Using a wooden skewer, make a hole for inserting a dried flower stem. (**Photo 5**)
2. Insert the stem in the hole in the foam. (**Photo 6**)
3. Apply hot glue around the stem to secure it in place. (**Photo 7**)

Covering Foam:

I like to use moss to cover any exposed foam. Attach the moss to the surface of the foam by applying a few dots of hot glue to the foam and pressing the moss in place. You can also use some thick white craft glue or floral pins to hold the moss in place on the foam.

Making Hangers

When making designs that will be hung on a wall or door, you can make your own hangers using floral wire.

1. Cut a piece of wire 4" to 10" long.
2. Fold the wire in half and twist.
3. Shape the twisted wire into a U-shape. Insert the ends in the back of the foam base at the top of the design.
4. Use hot glue to secure the wire ends to the foam. Cover the exposed glue with moss.

Photo 5 – Using a wooden skewer to make a hole for inserting a dried flower stem.

Photo 6 – Inserting the stem in the hole in the foam.

Photo 7 – Applying hot glue around the stem to secure it in place.

USING DRIED FLOWERS
IN YOUR HOME

Setting a Style

Before starting to create a design, think of the effect you are trying to achieve or the mood you are trying to create. Do you want a design that's formal or informal? Flamboyant? Antique or modern? Selecting and combining different elements that have similar characteristics will create a unified overall impression.

For example, the relaxed, romantic English country garden style is achieved with bunches of flowers grouped together (sometimes still wrapped in the rubber bands in which they were dried). The modern minimalist style combines strong, dramatic, and simple textures and shapes to catch the eye. A rustic country style might incorporate woven baskets, barn wood, or old jugs as containers – the older and more rustic, the better.

If a container is visible, make sure it is worth being seen. If you cannot find one you like, try adapting something you already have with a new painted finish or embellishments.

Using Color

Because a floral design is normally used to coordinate color schemes within the room and is usually a focal point to attract attention, be aware of the dominant colors in the room. Select some flowers that are slightly brighter and some slightly darker, and put in a few flowers in contrasting colors to make the arrangement stand out among the furnishings.

People react to colors both physically and emotionally. Yellows, oranges, and reds are advancing, "hot" colors that catch the attention. Greens, blues, and violets are perceived as receding or "cool." Red is aggressive and powerful but also romantic. Blue is the color of intellect – calm, cool, and reflective. Yellow can be harsh and aggravate the emotions, while green is considered balanced and at ease with itself.

Changing Colors with the Seasons

Use the colors of nature to guide you when creating seasonal arrangements.

In spring, the light is soft, and the colors are the lime greens of new foliage, the yellow of daffodils, lilacs and blues of violets and hyacinths. Some of these flowers are difficult to air dry, but experimenting with silica gel may create some pleasant surprises.

In summer, the sunshine is intense and so are the colors – bright pinks, powerful blues and bright whites, rich dark greens, fresh yellows, lilacs, and reds. The choice of summer flower varieties is extensive; hydrangea, larkspur, and all of the grasses are but a few possibilities for summer designs.

Autumn brings in new shades of browns, oranges, and golds. Sunflowers and grains are all readily available for fabulous displays.

With winter comes the icy look of bare twigs, dark evergreens, and native seasonal berries, cones, and nuts.

Understanding Scale, Contrast
& Color

A small table centerpiece can be intricately designed to showcase individual flower heads, but large scale displays that are viewed from a distance need to incorporate larger individual blooms or have groupings of several stems. Contrasts of texture, tone and color are important and the stronger they are the more the display will stand out. Just remember that the detail of dark colors may be lost as shadows. Yellow, orange, and white flowers are most visible from a distance.

The eye is drawn to elements that are strong in scale or texture so these elements need to be balanced along with the colors. Choose materials that provide one of these functions: focus, background, direction, texture, or volume. TIP: Sometimes one element can provide multiple functions. You may only need a small variety of flowers and foliage to make your displays complete.

Focal point material, which is usually the largest and heaviest element in a design, must appear balanced. The focal point material is usually placed near the container's rim, centrally placed or just off center – depending on the effect desired. With the addition of smaller and lighter materials, the eye is drawn upward and outward through the design.

Repeating elements produce pleasing eye movements. Use them as radiating lines from the center, creating visual pathways that move the eye from the focal area to the edges of the design and back.

The height and proportion of a design can be determined simply by using your eyes to decide if the elements are pleasing or not. You can see when the height and proportion are correct; if they are not, your eyes will tell you. TIP: Use this rule: The height of an arrangement above the container should be 1-1/2 to 2 times the height of the container.

These same basic principles apply to creating pressed flower designs, but on a smaller scale – you will make the same design decisions using smaller numbers of flowers and leaves. To give pressed designs dimension, mix in different shades of greens and layer flowers and background materials. With smaller scale designs, it's necessary to carefully select materials to coordinate with the surroundings and complement the theme and style of other elements that make up the design.

If you love flowers and have the confidence to be creative, you can easily master the skills to create your own beautiful dried and pressed floral designs. Only by observation and experimentation will you learn how the plant materials react to light or how to successfully combine colors.

No matter how long or hard you may work on a dried design, it will not last forever. Try to change the flowers and explore new ideas to update it before it becomes faded.

DRIED FLOWER ARRANGEMENTS

Use dried flowers and foliage to brighten dark corners and bring the outdoors inside your home. Most designs can be easily adapted to fit into any style simply by changing the container or substituting some of the flowers or leaves. These designs illustrate ideas for using a variety of flowers (sunflowers, roses, hydrangeas, yarrow), plus ferns, leaves, cattails, evergreens, rose hips, feathers, artichokes, mushrooms, herbs, and chili peppers. Use the supplies lists and instructions as guides for creating displays with your own personal touches.

Roses & Candles

Instructions on pages 38 & 39

ROSES & CANDLES

Pictured on pages 36 & 37

This beautiful arrangement would make a very romantic centerpiece for a Valentine's table. Or, add a gold bow around the base and use it for a Christmas centerpiece. It is very versatile and easy to put together.

An old painted box holds red roses and candles in small pots for a glowing centerpiece. You can use a deeper box to give more height to the arrangement (like the one on the preceding page) or a shallow, tray-type box (like the one used in the photos, *opposite,*) for an arrangement with a lower profile.

SUPPLIES

Container & Base:

• 1 rustic black wooden box, 12" long

• 2 terra cotta pots, 6" diameter

• 4 Plastic foam blocks (such as Styrofoam® brand), 2" x 4" x 8"

Plant Materials:

• 35 red roses on stems

• 1 bunch wild rose hips

• 1 bunch boxwood

• Green reindeer moss

• 5 medium pine cones

Tools & Other Supplies:

• 7 red candles, 6" tall

• Acrylic craft paint – Red

• Paper towels

• Low-temp glue gun and glue sticks

• Stem cutters

• Serrated knife

• Floral wire

INSTRUCTIONS

Designer's Tip: If you're going to be moving the arrangement, attach picks to the pine cones to hold them in place.

1. Use pieces of paper towels to randomly apply red paint to the wooden box. Allow to dry.
2. Using the knife, trim the plastic foam to fit inside the pots. Use hot glue to attach one pot in the back corner of the box and the other one in the front corner at an angle. (**Photo 1**)
3. Cut the rest of the plastic foam to fit the bottom of the box around the pots. Secure with hot glue.
4. Use hot glue to cover the foam in the tray with green reindeer moss. (**Photo 2**)
5. Wrap candles with floral wire to make a bundle. Use hot glue to secure the candles in the center of the back pot. (**Photo 3**) Fill the edges with green reindeer moss.
6. Trim the stems of the roses to 3" and insert them into the pot in the front of the box. (**Photo 4**)
7. Use hot glue to secure two pine cones on the right side and three pine cones in the back left side of the box. (**Photo 5**)
8. Trim the boxwood pieces so they are between 3" and 7" long. (**Photo 6**) Insert them between the pine cones and around the pots allowing the longer stems to extend horizontally on the left and right sides of the box. Insert several longer stems around the pot with the candles in the back of the box. (**Photo 7**)
9. Trim the stems of the rose hips to between 3" and 7" long. Insert them around the front pot (the one with the roses), allowing them to extend over the sides of the box. Insert the remaining rose hips between the boxwood and beside the pot with the candles.
10. Stand back from the box to check the positioning of the stems. Reposition them, if needed. ❑

Photo 1 – The plastic foam is arranged in the box and the pots, and the pots are glued in place.

Photo 2 – The plastic foam is covered with reindeer moss.

Photo 5 – The pine cones are glued in place.

Photo 3 – The candles are glued in one pot.

Photo 6 – The boxwood pieces are trimmed.

Photo 4 – The roses are inserted in the other pot.

Photo 7 – Longer boxwood stems are inserted around the pot with the candles.

Photo 1 – Dipping pieces of tissue paper in the glue-and-water mixture.

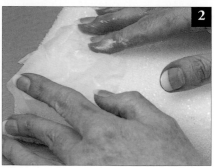

Photo 2 – Pressing the tissue on the plastic foam sheet.

Photo 3 – Stamping words with black ink on the tissue-covered plastic foam sheet.

WOODSY MIRROR

Recycle a makeup mirror to create a natural and unique wallhanging. Decorate it with greenery and use tissue paper and rubber stamps to add favorite words or sayings.

SUPPLIES

Base Supplies:
- Plastic foam sheet, 8" x 12", 1-1/2" thick
- 1 mirror, 3" x 4"
- Acrylic craft paints – Raw Umber, Raw Sienna
- Stamp pad with black ink
- Acrylic stamping medium
- 1 sheet white tissue paper
- Scrap of decorative paper
- Rubber stamps – Italian words, postage images
- Brown floral wire
- White craft glue
- Low-temp glue gun and glue sticks

Plant Materials:
- 2 cedar stems
- 2 feather fern stems
- 6 bay leaves on stems
- 1 mushroom
- Light green reindeer moss

Tools:
- Stem cutters
- Disposable plastic bowl
- Small paint brush
- Wire cutters
- Serrated knife
- *Optional:* Hair dryer

INSTRUCTIONS

Prepare the Base:

1. Use the serrated knife to trim the plastic foam sheet to 7" x 9".

2. Mix one part craft glue with two parts water in the disposable plastic bowl.

3. Tear the tissue into small pieces. Dip the tissue pieces in the glue-and-water mixture. (**Photo 1**) Press the tissue pieces over the top and sides of the plastic foam sheet until the plastic foam is completely covered. (**Photo 2**) Allow dry completely.

4. Use white craft glue to secure any loose pieces of tissue. Cover the back of the plastic foam sheet with decorative paper. Let dry.

5. Add water to raw sienna paint until the paint is a wash consistency. Brush the diluted paint over the tissue-covered plastic foam. Then use the brush to lightly apply water over the paint to smooth it out and blend. Allow to dry completely. TIP: Use a hair dryer to speed drying time.

6. Mix raw umber paint with stamping medium. Use the rubber stamps with black ink or the raw umber paint mix to randomly stamp Italian words and postage stamp images on the tissue-covered plastic foam sheet. (**Photo 3**)

7. Cut a 3" piece of brown wire and form a hanger. Insert the ends of the hanger into the top back side of the tissue-covered plastic foam sheet. Secure the ends of the hanger with hot glue. Cover the glue with green reindeer moss.

Make the Arrangement:

8. Use hot glue to secure the mirror to the center of the front of the paper-covered plastic foam sheet.

9. Cover the edges of the mirror with small pieces of green reindeer moss.

10. Glue the mushroom below the mirror. Cover the bottom with green reindeer moss.

11. Trim the cedar pieces to 9". Use hot glue to attach them at the sides of the mirror.

12. Trim the fern pieces to 6". Use hot glue to attach them on top of the cedar.

13. Use hot glue to attach three bay leaves on each side of the mushroom. ❑

SEASIDE POTS

Here's an idea for using the seashells and other treasures you've collected at the beach. Combine them with some weathered clay pots, candles, and roses, and display your collection on your dining room table.

SUPPLIES

Containers & Base:

• 3 Weathered clay pots, 5" diameter, with saucers

• 2 Plastic foam blocks, each 2" x 4" x 8"

Plant Materials:

• 40 pale yellow long-stemmed roses

• 2 pale yellow dried rose heads

• Natural reindeer moss

Tools & Other Supplies:

• Small piece of fish netting

• Raffia

• Assorted seashells and starfish

• Pale yellow pillar candles – two 4" x 3", one 4" x 4"

• Scissors

• Stem cutters

• Low-temp glue gun and glue sticks

• Serrated knife

Instructions continued on page 44

SEASIDE POTS
Continued from page 42

INSTRUCTIONS

Prepare the Parts:

1. Use the serrated knife to cut three 2" tall pieces from one plastic foam block to fit inside all three pots. Glue the plastic foam inside the pots.

2. Glue the two smaller candles on top of the Foam in two pots.

3. Cut a 1" tall piece of Foam. Glue it on top of the foam in the third pot.

4. Glue the larger candle in the third pot.

5. Cut the other plastic foam block in half. Use hot glue to cover one of the foam pieces with natural reindeer moss.

6. Glue small pieces of moss in the pots around the candles.

7. Separate the long-stemmed roses into four groups of ten roses. Position the roses to form two X-shapes. Tie each X-shape together in the center with raffia bow.

8. Glue the two rose heads beside the raffia bow on one X-shape.

Assemble the Arrangement:

9. Spread the netting on the table top. Place the moss-covered Foam block in the center.

10. Place the pot and saucer with the larger candle on top of the block. Place a pot and saucer with a smaller candle on each side, using the photo as a guide.

11. Lean the rose X-shape with the rose heads against the fronts of the pots. Place the second rose X-shape against the backs of the pots.

12. Use hot glue to adhere one seashell to the moss below each candle and two small seashells in the saucer of the center pot.

13. Place the remaining seashells and starfish around the bottoms of the pots on the netting. ❏

MAKING FAUX WEATHERED POTS

Here's how to make new pots look weathered. This technique can also be used on wood, cardboard, or paper for a worn leather look.

You'll Need:

Clay pot(s)

3 cans spray paint – 2 shades of green, dark wood tone

Sand or baby powder

Here's How:

1. Wet the surface of the pot with water and spray randomly with all three spray paints. Be sure the pot is wet when you're spraying.

2. While the paint is still wet, sprinkle some sand or baby powder over it. Blow gently on the powder to separate it and to create the look of lichen moss. Let dry. ❏

MAGNOLIA CENTERPIECE

Pictured on pages 46 & 47

Magnolia leaves are versatile and make wonderful companions for dried flowers and botanicals. They work well in everyday designs and create beautiful contrasts for red or white poinsettias, roses, or hydrangeas. Use them in rustic metal or iron containers to create a sophisticated look for your table or mantel.

SUPPLIES

Container & Base:
- Rectangular pressed metal container with iron stand, 9" x 21" x 6"
- 7 Plastic foam blocks, each 2" x 4" x 8"

Plant Materials:
- 8 magnolia branches with leaves
- 4 cream and pink hydrangea bunches
- 4 natural artichokes on stems
- 1 large bunch red tortum
- 1 small bunch autumn tortum
- Green reindeer moss

Tools & Other Supplies:
- 2 beaded tassels with cording, 7" long
- Stem cutters
- Serrated knife
- 5 wooden skewers, 6" long
- Floral pins
- Low-temp glue gun and glue sticks

INSTRUCTIONS

1. Use the serrated knife to trim the plastic foam blocks to fit inside the container. Use wooden skewers to secure the blocks on the top to the ones in the bottom of the container.
2. Use hot glue to cover the exposed plastic foam with green reindeer moss.
3. Tie the cording between the tassels into loose knots. Use floral pins to secure the tassels and cording so they drape down one side of the container.
4. Trim the magnolia stems to about 9". Insert them around the outer edges of the container, allowing the stems to extend over the edges.
5. Trim the artichoke stems to about 2". Insert them in a cluster in the center.
6. Trim the stems of the hydrangeas to about 4". Insert them on either side of the container close to the artichokes.
7. Trim several red tortum to about 9". Insert them between the leaves in the center of each magnolia stem.
8. Trim several red and autumn tortum to about 4". Insert them around the hydrangeas and artichokes. ❏

MAGNOLIA CENTERPIECE

Instructions on page 45

COUNTRY WINDOW BOX

I combined an old wooden window sash and a simple rectangular wooden box to make a unique container for dried flowers and leaves. Roses and hydrangea create a romantic, vintage look. The arrangement can be used as a wall hanging or can be propped against a wall or positioned on a table.

SUPPLIES

Container & Base:

- 1 six-pane wooden sash
- Rectangular wooden box (the same width as the window)
- 4 Plastic foam blocks, each 2" x 4" x 8"
- Wood screws

Plant Materials:

- 17 yellow roses
- 6 red roses
- 16 pink roses
- 10 bunches blue and green hydrangea
- 6 curly fern stems

Tools & Other Supplies:

- Stem cutters
- Green floral tape
- Floral wire
- Wire cutters
- Serrated knife
- Screw driver

INSTRUCTIONS

1. Screw the window sash to the back of the wooden box.
2. Use the serrated knife to trim the plastic foam blocks to fit inside the wooden box.
3. Trim the hydrangea stems to 4" to 6". Insert them in the plastic foam around the front and sides of the box.
4. Trim the rose stems to 12" to 14". Insert the red roses and six yellow roses in a group in the center back side of the box.
5. Insert seven yellow roses in a group on one side of the other roses.
6. Insert seven pink roses in a group on the other side of the roses in the center.
7. Insert the remaining roses among the rose groupings, filling any gaps.
8. Trim the fern stems to 8" to 10". Insert two on each side of the box next to the window and one on the left front side between the hydrangea. Insert the remaining fern stem on the right front side of the box. ❏

THISTLE & ARTICHOKE ARRANGEMENT

The beautiful burnished colors of these dried materials are enhanced by the brilliant copper container. This arrangement will add a warm glow to any room in your home.

Thistles grow wild and can be found in most woodland areas. They add interesting textures to arrangements and work well with contrasting textures of smooth leaves and grasses. Mix them with similar colors or combine them with a variety of different shades of browns, golds, and oranges to create a warm, natural looking design.

SUPPLIES

Container & Base:
• Copper container with iron ring handles, 8" tall
• 3 Plastic foam blocks, each 2" x 4" x 8"

Plant Materials:
• 6 natural thistles on stems
• 3 natural artichokes on stems
• 3 black sorghum stems
• 12 gold, orange, and green salal
• 1 small bunch autumn tortum
• 1 bunch natural grass stems
• 2 or 3 natural branches, 32" tall (If you can find some with moss growing on them this will make your arrangement more interesting.)
• Natural reindeer moss
• Green reindeer moss

Tools & Other Supplies:
• Low-temp glue gun and glue sticks
• Serrated knife

INSTRUCTIONS

Prepare the Container:

1. Use the serrated knife to trim the plastic foam blocks as needed to secure them inside the container. Secure one piece of plastic foam on top of the others, allowing it to extend about 3" above the top of the container.

2. Use hot glue to cover the exposed plastic foam with natural reindeer moss.

Create Arrangement:

3. Insert the natural branches into the center of the moss-covered plastic foam piece. (*Note: if you can't find branches tall enough, you can extend them with wire since much of the bottom half of the branches will be covered with plant material.*)

4. Trim one black sorghum stem to about 30". Insert it behind the two branches. Trim the other two black sorghum stems to about 22". Insert them on either side of the other sorghum stem. Save some of the green grass blades to use later.

5. Trim two natural grass stems to 18" and one to 17". Insert them around the branches in the center.

6. Trim two thistles to about 12", one to about 15", and three to about 10". Insert the tallest one in the center behind the branches. Insert the two 12" thistles on either side of the branches. Insert the three 10" thistles in front of the branches at different heights.

7. Trim the artichoke stems to about 4". Insert them close together in front of the three thistles.

8. Trim the tortum to various lengths – 8" to 2". Insert the taller ones among the thistles and branches and the shorter ones among the artichokes.

9. Trim the salal to various lengths – 17", 12", and 2". Insert the tall ones in the back behind the branches. Insert the 12" stems on the sides. Insert one stem in the center near the branches and place the 2" stems at the front beside the thistles.

10. Trim the green sorghum grass blades 17" to 12". Insert them among the branches and thistles.

11. Stand back from the design to check the positioning of the stems. Adjust as desired.

12. Glue several small pieces of green reindeer moss beside the artichokes on top of the natural moss. ❏

YARROW & FERN MIRROR

Add a woodsy flavor to your décor by trimming a wooden framed mirror with dried plant material. This makes a beautiful statement in an entry or bathroom. At first glance, this mirror appears to have been outdoors for a long time. You can create this same illusion by drying materials from your yard or by gathering a few things while walking in the woods.

For best results, choose a mirror with a wide frame to best display your florals. Random spritzes of antiquing spray on the frame and the edges of the mirror add to the aged look. If you leave the stems long on the florals, keep the leaves attached, and position the plant materials similar to the way they naturally grow, you can give any frame this rustic, overgrown look. Using some vines to wrap the hanger wire is an interesting option.

SUPPLIES

Base:

• Mirror with wide wooden frame, 22" x 25" (The mirror I chose had some subtle decorative painting of pansies around the frame. I made the painting even more subtle by adding antiquing spray to the frame.)

Plant Materials:

• 16 stems oregano
• 6 stems yellow yarrow
• 4 mushrooms
• 13 fan fern stems
• Green reindeer moss

Tools & Other Supplies:

• Stem cutters
• Antiquing spray
• Low-temp glue gun and glue sticks

INSTRUCTIONS

1. Following the antiquing spray manufacturer's instructions for use, randomly spray the mirror frame. Allow some of the spray to cover areas around the edges of the mirror glass. Allow to dry completely.

2. Use small dots of hot glue to secure the oregano stems on both sides of the mirror frame. Trim the bottoms of the stems if they extend below the bottom of the frame.

3. Use small dots of hot glue to secure the ferns around the bottoms of the oregano stems on both sides. Position the longer ones on the outside and angle the smaller ones toward the mirror.

4. Trim the stems of the yarrow to 4". Use hot glue to attach them to the bottom corners and top center of the frame. Secure three yarrow stems at the bottom center.

5. Use hot glue to secure one mushroom on each bottom corner and two mushrooms at the top center.

6. Use hot glue to secure small pieces of oregano and green reindeer moss around the mushrooms and yarrow.

7. Cover any exposed glue with pieces of moss. ❑

WILDFLOWER TOOLBOX TOTE

This casual arrangement makes it appear that you have just gathered the flowers from a hilltop field. Arrangements like this add a homey feel to your décor.

Old barn wood containers like this toolbox work perfectly for creating natural displays of dried marigolds, Queen Anne's lace, and coneflowers. The handle adds a wonderful functional appearance and allows you to easily move your flowers from one room to another.

Instructions appear on page 56

WILDFLOWER TOOLBOX TOTE

Pictured on page 54

SUPPLIES

Container & Base:
- Barnwood container with handle
- 3 Plastic foam blocks, 2" x 4" x 8"

Plant Materials:
- 2 bunches (20 stems) Queen Anne's lace
- 28 purple coneflowers
- 18 yellow marigolds
- 18 orange marigolds
- 28 yellow daisies
- Green reindeer moss

Tools & Other Supplies:
- Low-temp glue gun and glue sticks
- Stem cutters
- Serrated knife
- Floral pins

INSTRUCTIONS

1. Use the serrated knife to trim the plastic foam blocks to fit inside the container.

2. Use hot glue to cover the top of the foam with green reindeer moss.

3. Place the two bunches of Queen Anne's Lace horizontally in opposite directions in the front and back of the box. Secure them in the foam with floral pins and glue.

4. Trim fourteen coneflowers to between 12" and 18". Insert them in the center front of the box. Insert the remaining coneflowers – without trimming them – in a bunch behind the others.

5. Trim eight orange marigolds to between 12" and 18". Insert them at the left front side of the box. Insert the remaining orange marigolds – without trimming them – in a bunch behind the others.

6. Trim eight yellow marigolds to between 12" and 18". Insert them at the right front of the box. Insert the remaining yellow marigolds – without trimming them – in a bunch behind the others.

7. Trim fourteen daisies to between 10" and 18". Insert them in small bunches to fill the gaps between the other flowers. Insert the remaining daisies in small bunches – without trimming them – behind the shorter flowers.

8. Stand back from the box and observe the arrangement. Reposition any of the flowers to balance the design or to fill obvious gaps. ❏

LAVENDER TRIOS

Pictured on page 58

Lavender Pots

SUPPLIES

- Painted metal triple pot with handle, 8" x 3-1/2"
- 1 bunch lavender stems (or more, depending upon the size of your pots)
- Stem cutters

INSTRUCTIONS

1. Divide lavender stems to make three equal bunches. You will need enough stems to nicely fill each pot.

2. Trim the stems of each bunch to between 9" and 10", or to the length needed for the size pot you have chosen. Trim the stems so the flowers begin just at the rim of the pot

3. Place the stems loosely inside the three pots. ❏

Lavender Balls

SUPPLIES

- Plastic foam balls – two 3", one 2-1/2", two 2"
- 8 oz. lavender buds (3 cups)
- Large plastic bag
- Spray adhesive
- Disposable gloves
- Raffia
- Scissors

INSTRUCTIONS

1. Place the lavender buds inside the large plastic bag.

2. Read the manufacturer's instructions for using the spray adhesive. Working one ball at a time and wearing disposable gloves, hold one ball and spray it with adhesive.

3. Immediately drop the ball into the bag of lavender buds. Use both hands to press the buds onto the ball.

4. Re-apply the adhesive and buds until the ball is completely covered.

5. Repeat steps 2, 3, and 4 for the remaining balls. Allow the adhesive to dry completely before proceeding.

6. Wrap one 3" ball and one 2-1/2" ball with raffia and tie a bow on each. Trim the ends of the raffia as desired. ❏

LAVENDER TRIOS

Instructions appear on page 57

Use lavender stems and buds to perfume the air with one of nature's most pleasant and relaxing aromas. Dried lavender keeps its fragrance for years. Simply crush a few buds to release its intoxicating aroma. Lavender scent is known to relieve stress and is often used as an aid in sleeping. Place it by your bedside to ensure a restful nights sleep.

Here, I've placed loose stems of dried lavender in three small pots and covered small plastic foam balls with lavender buds to create this display. You can use a trio of connected pots as I have or fill individual pots and arrange them on a tray.

You can arrange your lavender pots and covered balls together or place them here and there in several rooms to indulge your sense of smell with the wonderful scent of lavender.

Designer's Tip: Use the white, more porous foam balls for this project. They work much better with spray adhesive than dry floral foam balls.

SPECIMENS UNDER GLASS

Search through your treasures for an old rusted lantern or buy a new one – a lantern is a great container for dried materials and it makes a wonderful changing display for nature's treasures. You can swap out fall leaves and cones for spring nests and grasses or display candles and evergreens for the holidays. Add your favorite photos for special occasions.

SUPPLIES

Container & Base:
- Metal and glass lantern, 16-1/2" tall, 6" square
- Plastic foam block, 1" x 4" x 4"

Plant Materials:
- 2 acorns
- 1 large pine cone
- 1 twig with an attached acorn
- 1 bay leaf stem
- 2 bay leaves
- 1 bunch cream hydrangea
- 1 bracken fern stem
- Green reindeer moss

Tools & Other Supplies:
- Low-temp glue gun and glue sticks
- Serrated knife

INSTRUCTIONS

1. Use the serrated knife to cut a 1" x 1" x 4" piece of plastic foam.
2. Use hot glue to cover one of the 4" sides and all of the 1" sides with green reindeer moss.
3. Trim the bay leaf stem to 8". Insert it in the back side of the plastic foam piece. Place the plastic foam piece with the stem in the back of the bottom of the lantern.
4. Glue the pine cone to the front of the plastic foam piece.
5. Trim the twig with the acorn to 8". Glue the bottom of the twig to the top right side of the pine cone, angling it to the left so it touches the side of the lantern. Cover the glue with green reindeer moss.
6. Glue the bay leaves in the bottom right side of the lantern.
7. Trim the fern to 4". Glue it on top of the bay leaves.
8. Glue the acorns on top of the fern.
9. Trim the hydrangea stem to 2". Place it on the left side. ❑

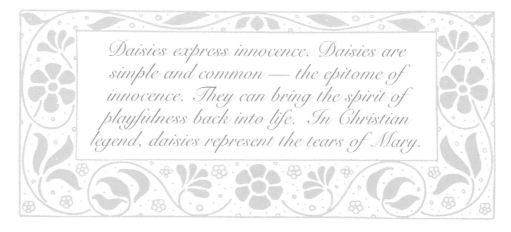

Daisies express innocence. Daisies are simple and common — the epitome of innocence. They can bring the spirit of playfulness back into life. In Christian legend, daisies represent the tears of Mary.

ARTFUL GOURDS

The natural colors and shapes of gourds make them perfect bases for creating unique displays. Simply position a small twig wreath over the top and insert colorful leaves, stems, cuttings from your garden, or feathers.

SUPPLIES

- 2 natural, unfinished gourds – different colors
- 6 fall color laurel or salal stems
- 2 twig wreaths, 6" diameter
- 6 pheasant feathers – three 21" to 23", three 16" to 18"

Optional:

- Low-temp glue gun and glue sticks
- Green reindeer moss

INSTRUCTIONS

1. Position the twig wreaths over the tops of the gourds.
2. Trim the laurel or salal stems to between 8" and 12". Insert three stems between each wreath and gourd.
3. Insert the three longer pheasant feathers between the wreath and the larger gourd.
4. Insert the three shorter pheasant feathers between the wreath and the smaller gourd.
5. *Option:* Use hot glue to secure the wreaths, stems, and feathers to the gourds. Cover any exposed glue with reindeer moss. ❏

Designer's Tip: If you would like to reuse your gourds later, do not use glue to secure the stems, wreaths, or feathers.

CATTAILS & PUSSY WILLOWS

Cattails and pussy willows can usually be found growing wild in low lying areas. They blend well with contrasting and more intense colors like yarrow and look right at home in a rusted metal or rustic wooden container.

SUPPLIES

Container & Base:
- Rusted metal vase with wood trim, 10" tall
- 2 Plastic foam blocks, 2" x 4" x 8"

Plant Materials:
- 9 dark brown large cattails
- 14 light brown small cattails
- 22 pussy willows
- 1 small bunch of 14" pieces of honeysuckle vine
- 6 stems yellow yarrow
- 7 artichokes
- 10 grapevine stems
- 10 stems small brown oak leaves
- *Optional:* Green reindeer moss

Tools & Other Supplies:
- Brown floral wire
- Wire cutters
- Stem cutters
- Serrated knife
- *Optional:* Low-temp glue gun and glue sticks

INSTRUCTIONS

1. Use the serrated knife to trim the plastic foam blocks as needed to secure them inside the vase. Trim the plastic foam even with the top of the vase.
2. Trim the pussy willows to between 20" and 26". Trim the cattails to between 12" and 28".
3. Insert the pussy willows in the center of the vase.
4. Insert the larger cattails among the pussy willows. Fill in around them with smaller cattails.
5. Separate the honeysuckle vine into two bunches. Wrap the ends of each punch with small pieces of brown wire. Insert the ends of the wires in the back of the vase on each side and position them so they drape over the edges and wrap around to the front of the vase.
6. Trim the stems of the artichokes to 4". Insert them around the edge of the vase.
7. Trim the yarrow stems to between 6" and 12". Insert them in a group at center front.
8. Trim the grapevine stems to between 20" and 26". Insert them among the cattails and pussy willows.
9. Trim the oak leaf stems to between 10" and 12". Insert them around the bottoms of the grapevine stems, filling any obvious gaps.
10. Stand back from the vase and check the positions of the stems. Adjust as desired.
11. *Option:* Use hot glue to attach small pieces of green reindeer moss between the artichokes and to secure the stems and artichokes in the container. ❏

SUMMER SUNFLOWER MEMORIES

Each sunflower has a unique personality. They are so easy (and a lot of fun) to grow from seeds. Their shapes may change dramatically as they dry, and they usually do not require companion flowers to make a striking arrangement. I've grouped them here with leaves and some curly twigs.

SUPPLIES

Container & Base:
- Basket vase, 14" tall
- 3 Plastic foam blocks, 2" x 4" x 8"
- Stones or marbles

Plant Materials:
- 11 large sunflowers
- 8 curly willow twigs
- 8 stems laurel or salal leaves
- 6 stems baby's breath (gypsophilia)

Tools & Other Supplies:
- Serrated knife

INSTRUCTIONS

1. Fill the bottom of the vase with stones or marbles for stability.
2. Use the knife to trim the plastic foam blocks as needed so they can be inserted in the vase. For stability, wire or anchor the foam with glue.
3. Trim the sunflower stems to between 16" and 20". Insert them in the foam inside the vase, positioning them to form a balanced shape. Leave some space between the flowers.
4. Trim the twigs to between 20" and 36". Insert the twigs so they extend above the sunflowers.
5. Trim the laurel or salal stems to between 16" and 18". Insert them between the sunflowers close to the bottom of the stems.
6. Trim the baby's breath to 16" and 20". Insert them among the sunflowers.
7. Stand back from the vase and check the positioning of the sunflowers, leaves, twigs, and baby's breath. Reposition them as needed to create the desired shape. ❏

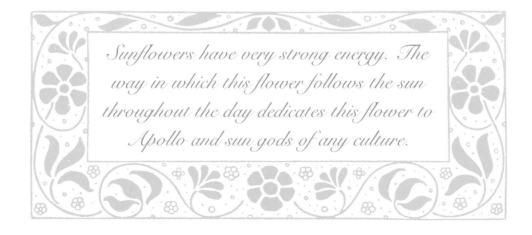

Sunflowers have very strong energy. The way in which this flower follows the sun throughout the day dedicates this flower to Apollo and sun gods of any culture.

ROSES & HYDRANGEAS

Antique containers are perfect for displaying dried flowers. Create your own unique and personal design by combining a variety of old containers in different shapes and finishes and then filling them with dried flowers from your garden.

SUPPLIES

Container & Base:
- Antique metal pitcher, 8" tall
- Plastic foam block, 2" x 4" x 8"

Plant Materials:
- 10 pink and cream roses
- 5 blue and purple hydrangea stems
- 2 cream and pink hydrangea stems

Tools & Other Supplies:
- 7 wooden floral picks
- 10 wire stems, 10" long
- Floral tape
- Stem cutters
- Serrated knife

Designer's Tip: To avoid damaging valuable containers, don't use glue to secure the plastic foam in the container. Use tape or floral clay instead.

INSTRUCTIONS

1. Use the knife to trim the plastic foam block to fit inside the pitcher.
2. Use floral tape to secure the rose heads to the stems. Trim the stems of the roses to between 8" and 10".
3. Insert the roses in the plastic foam, forming a mound in the center of the pitcher.
4. Attach the hydrangea stems to the wooden floral picks. Insert the blue and purple hydrangeas between the roses and the rim of the pitcher.
5. Insert the cream and pink hydrangeas behind the roses. ❑

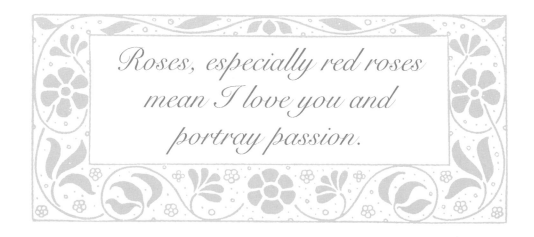

Roses, especially red roses mean I love you and portray passion.

LAVENDER & HYDRANGEAS

Try arranging hydrangea and lavender together inside glass vases, bowls, or other shapes, and use hydrangea petals and lavender buds to fill the bottom of the container. I used a twig wreath at the top of the vase, but if you'd like a romantic Victorian look, add some lace or ribbon to create a soft, feminine feeling.

SUPPLIES

Container:

• Flared glass vase, 12" tall

Plant Materials:

• 1 large bunch lavender stems
• 5 lavender-colored hydrangea stems, plus loose petals
• 8 oz. (1 cup) lavender buds
• 1 twig wreath, 6" diameter (or a size that fits the top of your vase – see Fig. 1)

Tools & Other Supplies:

• 1 wire stem, 15" long
• Floral adhesive tape
• Stem cutters
• Low-temp glue gun and glue sticks
• Floral wire

INSTRUCTIONS

1. Trim the lavender stems so the bunch is 12" tall. Use floral wire to wrap the stems 2" above the bottom of the bunch so the bunch stays together.
2. Fill the bottom of the vase with lavender buds.
3. Use small pieces of floral adhesive tape to secure the twig wreath at the top of the vase. (See Fig. 1)
4. Insert the wire stem in the center of the buds in the vase so it extends above the rim of the vase. Push the center of the lavender bunch on top of the stem. If needed, secure the bunch to the wire stem with floral wire.
5. Fill in around the base of the lavender bunch with loose hydrangea petals.
6. Trim the hydrangea stems to between 2" and 3". Use hot glue to secure them to the inside of the twig wreath. ❑

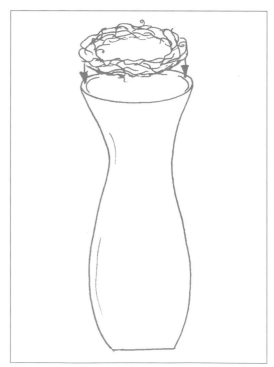

Fig. 1 – The twig wreath should sit just inside the rim of the vase.

ROSES & FERN FRONDS

You can have roses all year long when you use dried ones. This gorgeous display of roses and ferns is a classic pairing that will add elegance wherever it is displayed. Choose a classic style container for this arrangement.

After silica drying your roses, wire or tape them to long stems and combine them with dried bay, ferns, and laurel or salal stems to make this natural design in a classic fan shape.

Roses are available already dried for you at many florists or nurseries. Commercially dried roses may be freeze dried so that they retain their vivid colors when dried. They are fragile, so be careful when transporting and arranging them.

Instructions appear on pages 74 & 75

Designer's Tip: Using different colors of roses in groups makes the blooms appear larger than they really are.

ROSES & FERN FRONDS

Pictured on pages 72 & 73.

SUPPLIES

Container & Base:

• Octagonal metal container with lid, 6" tall, 7" wide

• 2 Plastic foam blocks, 2" x 4" x 8"

Plant Materials:

• 7 yellow and red roses

• 5 red roses

• 20 light green laurel or salal leaves

• 10 curly fern stems

• 12 feather fern stems

• 20 bay leaf stems

• 15 veronica stems

• Green reindeer moss

Tools & Other Supplies:

• Stem cutters

• 12 wire stems, 15" long

• Green floral tape

• Low-temp glue gun and glue sticks

• Serrated knife

INSTRUCTIONS

1. Use the serrated knife to trim the plastic foam blocks to fit inside the container. Allow one block to extend 4" above the top of the container.

2. Use hot glue to cover the block with green reindeer moss.

3. Trim the laurel or salal stems to between 14" and 17". Insert the nine longest stems in the foam at the back of the container to create the basic fan shape of the design. (Fig. 1)

4. Insert a second row of six shorter laurel or salal stems in front of the back row.

5. Place the remaining shorter laurel or salal stems at the front of the container, extending downward. (Fig. 2)

6. Trim the bay leaf stems to between 12" and 14". Insert them in the center of the fan shape among the salal. Allow them to extend downward, covering the top edges of the container.

7. Trim the fern stems to between 17" and 20". Insert them, spacing them evenly, around the fan shape of the design. Allow them to extend downward, covering the top edges of the container.

8. Stand back from the container and study the arrangement. Fill in the shape as desired with the remaining greenery.

9. Use green floral tape to secure the roses to individual stems.

10. Trim the stems of the yellow and red roses to between 8" and 15". Insert three of them together at center front. Insert three more at the upper left, using the photo as a guide. Insert one yellow and red rose at the upper right. (Fig. 3)

11. Insert three red roses on the right side and three more red roses on the left. (Fig. 4)

12. Insert several groups of veronica stems close to the rose groupings. ❏

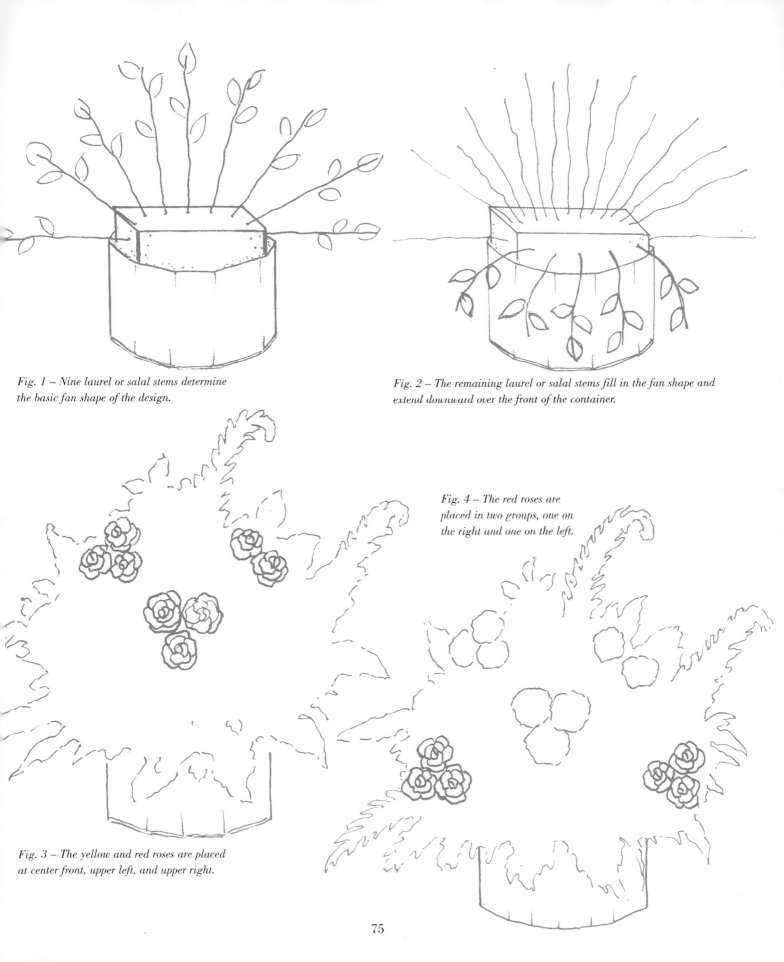

Fig. 1 – Nine laurel or salal stems determine
the basic fan shape of the design.

Fig. 2 – The remaining laurel or salal stems fill in the fan shape and
extend downward over the front of the container.

Fig. 4 – The red roses are
placed in two groups, one on
the right and one on the left.

Fig. 3 – The yellow and red roses are placed
at center front, upper left, and upper right.

FERNS & FEATHERS

Pheasant feathers add a striking point of interest to this simple grouping of greenery. Mix feathers, ferns, and laurel stems to create a natural display in a rustic container. You only need three different types of materials to create this quick and easy design.

SUPPLIES

Container & Base:

- Rusted green metal container with a recessed bottom, 8" tall, 7" wide
- Plastic foam block, 2" x 4" x 4"

Plant Materials:

- 10 pheasant feathers, 21" to 24"
- 20 light green laurel or salal leaves
- 20 curly fern stems
- Green reindeer moss

Tools & Other Supplies:

- Stem cutters
- Low-temp glue gun and glue sticks
- Serrated knife

INSTRUCTIONS

1. Turn the container upside down. Use the serrated knife to trim the plastic foam block the same size as the bottom of the container.
2. Glue the trimmed piece to the bottom of the container.
3. Glue green reindeer moss to cover the foam.
4. Insert the feathers in the top center of the foam.
5. Trim twelve laurel or salal stems to between 12" and 15".
6. Trim the ferns to between 7" and 10".
7. Insert the ferns around the feathers.
8. Insert the laurel or salal horizontally in the edges of the foam. Position some of the stems so they extend downward and partially cover the sides of the container.
9. Trim the remaining laurel or salal to between 4" and 6". Place them to fill any gaps between the ferns and the longer laurel or salal stems. ❑

CHILIES & HERBS WREATH

Dried herbs and spices liven up a room with their unique colors and scents. Try drying your own – you can buy them at farmers' markets in quantity – and combine them to create wreaths or swags or bouquets to hang on walls or doors.

Twig wreath forms are easy to find and make a good base for herbs and spices. You can also create your own twig wreaths with twigs or vines from your yard and floral wire.

INSTRUCTIONS

1. Cut the chili stems in pieces between 4" and 5" long. Insert them in small bunches around the wreath, positioning several longer pieces at the bottom outside edge of the wreath.
2. Use hot glue to secure the bay leaves around the wreath between the chilies.
3. Cut the rosemary stems in pieces between 4" and 6" long. Insert them around the wreath between the chilies and bay leaves. Position five longer stems in the bottom inside center of the wreath.
4. Stand back from the wreath and reposition the stems as needed to fill any obvious gaps.
5. *Option:* Remove the chilies and rosemary. Apply hot glue to the ends and reposition them on the wreath. ❏

SUPPLIES

Wreath Supplies:
- Twig wreath, 12"
- 12 red chili pepper stems with multiple peppers
- 8 rosemary stems
- 7 bay leaves

Tools & Other Supplies:
- Stem cutters
- Low-temp glue gun and glue sticks

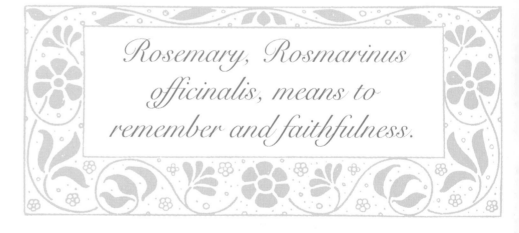

Rosemary, Rosmarinus officinalis, means to remember and faithfulness.

HYDRANGEA WREATH

Hydrangeas and ferns combine beautifully with natural twigs to make this simple wreath. It's quick and easy and makes a wonderful hostess or housewarming gift. Wreaths made with dried plant material are best displayed inside. Smaller wreaths like this one work well in small spaces but also look good on interior doors and over mantels.

SUPPLIES

Wreath Supplies:
- Loosely woven twig wreath, 16" diameter
- 5 green hydrangea stems
- 20 bracken fern stems

Tools & Other Supplies:
- Stem cutters
- *Optional:* Low-temp glue gun and glue sticks

INSTRUCTIONS

1. Trim the stems of the hydrangeas to 4". Insert them around the center and middle sections of the wreath.

2. Trim the individual fern stems to between 4" and 6". Insert them around the outside edges of the hydrangea, allowing them to radiate from the center and over the twigs of the base wreath.

3. Stand back from the wreath and reposition the stems as needed, filling any obvious gaps.

4. *Option:* Remove the hydrangeas and ferns, apply hot glue to the stems, and reposition them on the wreath. ❑

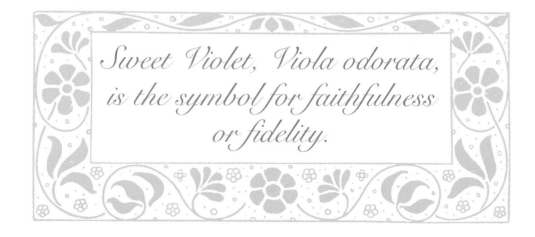

Sweet Violet, Viola odorata, is the symbol for faithfulness or fidelity.

LEAVES & ACORNS TOPIARY

Colored autumn leaves from your own backyard make an easy, economical tabletop solution. They are great to air-dry inside or preserve with glycerine. I like to use them to cover small foam balls (that's why I refer to them as "topiaries"). Display a grouping using your favorite containers, or make one large leaf-covered ball to fit in a single container. If you spray the leaves with sealer, they will last a long time. Many florists, gift shops, and craft shops carry pre-dried leaves.

SUPPLIES

Base & Container:
- Plastic foam ball, 4"
- 2 Plastic foam blocks, 2" x 4" x 8"
- Square metal container, 8"

Plant Materials:
- 40 stems with multiple oak leaves
- 8 twigs, each with 4 acorns

Tools & Other Supplies:
- Wooden skewer, 8" (or longer)
- Stem cutters
- Serrated knife
- Floral clay
- Thick white craft glue
- Low-temp glue gun and glue sticks

Designer's Tip: If you can't find any twigs with acorns attached, make your own. Find some interesting twigs and collect some pretty acorns. Glue the acorns to the twigs using hot glue.

INSTRUCTIONS

1. Cut the bottom third off a plastic foam ball so there is a flat side. (Fig. 1)
2. Glue the plastic foam blocks together with white glue to make a block the size of the container that comes to within 1" of the rim. Use the serrated knife to trim the foam as needed to fit into container. Glue the foam to the bottom of the container using floral clay.
3. Insert the wooden skewer in the center of the foam block. Trim the skewer so it extends 3" above the top of the container.
4. Use the stem cutters to trim the stems of the oak leaves to lengths between 5" and 7". Insert them in the plastic foam ball, leaving the bottom, flat side of the ball uncovered. *Option:* Apply hot glue to the stems before inserting them.
5. Trim the twigs with acorns to between 8" and 10". Insert them in the ball among the leaves, allowing them to extend above and outside of the leaves.
6. Put hot glue on the flat bottom of the leaf-covered foam ball. Push the bottom of the leaf-covered foam ball on the stick or skewer. ❑

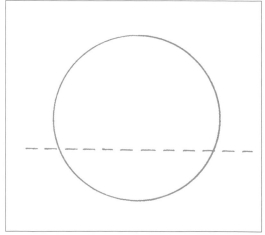

Fig. 1 – Cut bottom 1/3 from the plastic foam ball.

AUTUMN IN GLASS CYLINDERS

Glass containers are great ways to display dried materials, and it's easy to change the contents with the seasons. They also allow you to showcase your backyard finds. I love to display delicate petals such as dried rose petals in the summer. This idea works great for displaying your own dried potpourri. Collect all your broken and damaged dried flowers until you have enough to fill a container. These types of leftover petals make colorful displays.

Here, I've filled three different sizes of glass cylinders with cones, nuts, and leaves. Attached candles add a warm glow to the table.

SUPPLIES

Candle Holders:

- 3 glass cylinders, one 12" tall, one 11" tall, one 8-1/2" tall
- 3 candles, 3" in diameter or the size needed to fit into the cylinders you have purchased
- 3 wire candle holders to fit the tops of the cylinders

Dried Materials:

- 3 large pine cones
- Acorns
- Small nuts
- Small pine cones
- 6 autumn oak leaves
- Crape myrtle buds

INSTRUCTIONS

1. Fill the bottom half of the 12" cylinder with the large pine cones.
2. Fill the bottom half of the 11" cylinder with acorns and oak leaves.
3. Fill the bottom half of the 8-1/2" cylinder with the acorns, nuts, crape myrtle buds, and small pine cones.
4. Bend and adjust the wires of the metal candle holders to position the candles slightly above the materials in each cylinder.
5. Place the candles in the holders. ❏

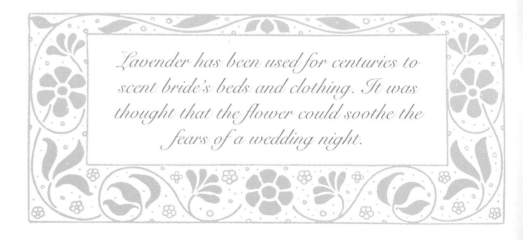

Lavender has been used for centuries to scent bride's beds and clothing. It was thought that the flower could soothe the fears of a wedding night.

HOLIDAY CHAIR SWAG

You can make chair decorations that coordinate with your centerpieces by using the same materials and adding ribbons to tie them to your chairs. The natural greens and reds create a traditional, festive look for family holidays. We've shown this swag on the front of the chair, which works well for chairs no one will be sitting in. For chairs where people will be sitting, position the swags on the backs of the chairs, where they will be visible as diners approach the table.

SUPPLIES

Swag Supplies:

- 2-1/2 yds. brown organza ribbon with gold wire edges, 1" wide
- 6 red rose heads
- 5 stems wild rose hips
- 4 magnolia leaves
- 3 cedar stems
- Green reindeer moss

Tools:

- Low temp glue gun and glue sticks
- Stem cutters
- Scissors

INSTRUCTIONS

1. To make the background for the swag, arrange the magnolia leaves, stem ends all in one direction with the stems overlapping. Use hot glue to attach them to each other.

2. Trim the cedar stems to between 10" and 12". Use hot glue to adhere them on top of the stems of the magnolia leaves.

3. Use hot glue to attach four rose heads in a vertical row down the center of the cedar stems. Add the other two on opposite sides of the row.

4. Trim the rose hips to between 3" and 6". Use hot glue to secure the longer ones between the roses at the bottom and the shorter ones between the roses at the top.

5. Use hot glue to cover the stems of the cedar and magnolia leaves with green reindeer moss.

6. Tie the center of the ribbon around the moss-covered stems. Position the swag on the chair back. Loop the ribbons around the back of a chair, then bring them back around to the side with the swag. Tie a bow at the top of the stems and allow the streamers to fall on either side of the swag.

7. Use scissors to trim the ends of the streamers to inverted V-shapes. ❑

JUNIPER, PINE CONES & LEAVES SWAG

A seasonal swag is a welcoming decoration for your door any time of the year, and making a swag is a simpler proposition than making a wreath. Here, evergreen boughs, pine cones, and fall leaves make a charming autumn display. The materials used for this swag will be fine used on an outside door.

SUPPLIES

Swag Supplies:
- 3 large preserved juniper stems with berries
- 5 pine cones
- 3 stems dried oak leaves
- 60" jute mesh wired-edge ribbon
- Green reindeer moss

Tools:
- Brown floral wire
- Low-temp glue gun and glue sticks
- Plastic foam block, 2" x 4" x 4"
- Floral pins
- Scissors
- Stem cutters
- Wire cutters

INSTRUCTIONS

1. Cover the plastic foam block with green reindeer moss, using hot glue.
2. Use the wire cutters to cut a 10" piece of brown wire. Fold the wire in half and twist the two pieces together. Shape the twisted piece to form a hanger. (Fig. 1)
3. Insert the ends of the wire hanger near the top of the back of the moss-covered block. Secure the ends with hot glue.
4. Trim two juniper stems to between 10" and 12". Insert one in the top on one side of the black and the other in the bottom of the other side of the block. Trim the other juniper stem to make two shorter pieces. Insert them in the top and bottom edges of the block opposite the other juniper stems. (Fig. 2)
5. Cut five 8" pieces of brown wire. Wrap one piece around the center of each pine cone. Pull the wire that circles the thick center stem of the pine cone and twist the wire ends together to form a stem for each pine cone.
6. Position the pine cones in the center of the plastic foam block, bending the wire stems and inserting them in the block with the larger ends of the pine cones flat against the block.
7. Trim the oak leaf stems to between 14" and 16". Insert them in the edges of the foam block behind the juniper stems so they extend below and above the juniper. Using Fig. 2 as a guide, place the first oak leaves stem behind juniper stem 1, extending upward. Add the other two stems behind juniper stems 2 and 4, extending downward.
8. Stand back from the swag. Reposition the leaves and juniper as needed to create a balanced look.
9. Wrap the jute ribbon around the pine cones, twisting the ribbon so it loosely circles the pine cones. Allow the ends to fall below the bottom edge of the block. Secure the ribbon to the block with floral pins and hot glue.
10. Fill in any gaps with small pieces of juniper and oak leaves, using hot glue to secure them. ❏

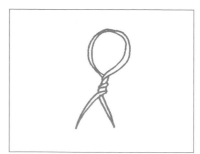

Fig. 1 – The hanger

Fig. 2 – Inserting the juniper stems.

EVERGREEN CANDLE CENTERPIECE

A rustic antique sugar mold holds candles and is surrounded by evergreen stems. Shiny round ornaments reflect the candlelight to create a warm, old-fashioned display for a holiday table or sideboard.

SUPPLIES

Container & Base:
- Wooden antique three-hole sugar mold
- Plastic foam sheet, 1" x 8" x 12"

Plant Materials:
- 8 cedar stems
- Green reindeer moss

Tools & Other Supplies:
- 10 red round ornaments with wires, 1-1/2" diameter
- 8 green round ornaments with wires, 1" diameter
- 10 red round ornaments with wires, 1" diameter
- 3 red votive candles, 2"
- Low-temp glue gun and glue sticks
- Stem cutters

INSTRUCTIONS

1. Center the sugar mold on top of the plastic foam sheet.
2. Use hot glue to cover the top of the foam around the sugar mold and the sides of the foam sheet with green reindeer moss.
3. Trim the cedar stems to between 4" and 12". Insert them in the moss-covered sheet around the base of the sugar mold. Allow the longer stems to extend beyond the sides of the base.
4. Insert the wires of five 1-1/2" red ornaments in a cluster in the foam base at the center front of the sugar mold.
5. Insert the other five 1-1/2" red ornaments in a cluster in the foam base at center back.
6. Surround each cluster with three small red ornaments.
7. Insert the wires of four green ornaments around the ornament cluster on the front. Insert the wires of two green ornaments around the cluster in the back.
8. Insert one green ornament and two small red ones on each end of the sugar mold.
9. Place the candles in the sugar mold.
10. Trim six 2" pieces of cedar and insert two around each candle. ❏

PRESERVED MAGNOLIAS HOLIDAY CENTERPIECE

This simple, quick holiday centerpiece showcases a collection of hand-blown glass ornaments and white pillar candles arranged among magnolia leaves on a mirrored silver tray. The pillar candles are placed on china saucers, which will catch any drips. Evergreen boughs form a base of greenery on the tray, and magnolia stems are arranged among the candles over the evergreens with the leaves overhanging the tray. A half dozen ornaments are tucked among the leaves. When the candles are lit, the flickering light illuminates the ornaments and the shiny surfaces of the magnolia leaves.

I wanted this arrangement to last only throughout the holiday season. I preserved the magnolia leaves and evergreen in glycerine, but did not leave them in the glycerine long enough to turn brown.

Designer's Tip: Since the centerpiece is made without glue or plastic foam, it would be difficult to move. Create the arrangement on the surface where you plan to display it.

PRESSED FLOWERS & LEAVES PROJECTS

Almost any flower and leaf can be pressed successfully so don't be afraid to press your own leaves and garden flowers. It is so easy. You may be surprised how wonderful they look when you open your press. Flat flowers work best for pressing, but you can also take flowers apart and press the flat part of them. For example, individual sections of petals from hydrangeas press beautifully. You can also pull off petals from roses and press them.

As the designs in this section show, pressed flowers and leaves look good no matter where you use them. They brighten areas in your home that need a small accent of color or a natural touch.

They can be successfully used under glass, or can be decoupaged onto a variety of surfaces. For personal gifts, experiment with layering them on decorative papers and add beads, buttons, and items that have special meaning.

See the "Tools & Supplies" section as well as the "Preserving Techniques" section for information about how to successfully press flowers.

Some Good Flowers & Leaves for Pressing

Aspen leaves

Aster

Clover leaves

Columbine

Coral bells

Coreopsis

Delphiniums

Ferns

Geranium leaves

Hydrangea (individual sections)

Ivy

Larkspur

Maidenhair ferns

Maple leaves

Pansies

Rose petals

Violas

Violets

FRAMED BOUQUET

If you have some empty frames, you can use them to display pressed flowers and leaves. Let the frame size, style, and shape be your inspiration. Layer leaves to create interesting shapes and coordinate the flower colors with the frame or room colors. You can make a variety of looks (e.g., rustic, contemporary, Victorian), depending on the style of frame and the type of dried material.

SUPPLIES

Arrangement Materials:

- Vintage tin frame with pink bead swag, 5" x 7"
- 1 pink columbine
- 2 artemisia leaves
- Background paper, 8" x 8" (pink scrapbook paper with vintage writing and postage cancellation shown here)

Tools & Other Supplies:

- Scissors
- Tweezers
- Acid-free glue
- Pencil
- Glass cleaner

BASIC INSTRUCTIONS

1. Remove the back and glass insert from the frame.
2. Place the glass insert over your chosen background paper and, using the pencil, trace around the glass shape on the paper. Use scissors to cut out the paper backing.
3. Clean and dry the glass.
4. Use the tweezers to position the dried materials. Place two artemisia leaves on the paper. Arrange the columbine on top.
5. Place the frame over the paper with the flowers and/or leaves. Adjust the placement of the dried materials as needed, making sure the dried materials are visible inside the frame.
6. Individually remove each leaf and flower. Place a small dot of glue on the back of each one and replace on the paper. Allow the glue to dry completely.
7. Place the glass, the paper with the leaves and flowers, and the frame backing in the frame. ❑

> **Designer's Tip:** When gluing pressed materials to papers, I recommend using acid-free adhesives to avoid any chemical reactions that may occur as time passes.

FRAMED FERN
& ASPEN

This is a wonderful way to display some of your pretty specimens. It is also a great way to get some pretty art on your walls.

SUPPLIES

Arrangement Materials:
- Rustic wood frame, 4" x 8"
- 2 mountain ferns
- 3 fall color aspen leaves
- Background paper, 8" x 8" (printed scrapbook paper of old newspaper clippings used here)

Tools & Other Supplies:
- Scissors
- Tweezers
- Acid-free glue
- Pencil
- Glass cleaner

INSTRUCTIONS

1. Remove the back and glass insert from the frame.
2. Place the glass insert over your chosen background paper and, using the pencil, trace around the glass shape on the paper. Use scissors to cut out the paper backing.
3. If needed, clean the glass.
4. Use the tweezers to position the dried materials. Position the aspen leaves to form a triangle in the center, then place a fern on each side.
5. Place the frame over the paper with the flowers and/or leaves. Adjust the placement of the dried materials as needed, making sure the dried materials are visible inside the frame.
6. Individually remove each leaf and flower. Place a small dot of glue on the back of each one and replace on the paper. Allow the glue to dry completely.
7. Place the glass, the paper with the leaves and flowers, and the frame backing in the frame. ❏

FLOWER BOOK

Use your pressed flowers to make fun little flower books and share them with your gardening friends. You could also use this idea to keep an annual record of the flowers you grew.

SUPPLIES

Book Materials:
- 1 sheet textured brown paper, 12" x 12"
- White copy paper
- Twine
- Antiquing paint
- Beads – 2 wood, 2 glass
- Acid-free glue
- Decoupage medium
- Sealer spray

Suggested Flowers for One Book:
- 3 violas with stems and leaves
- 1 viola bloom
- 6 yellow daisies
- 5 white daisies
- 4 large purple and yellow pansies
- 3 coreopsis with stems
- 2 pink and purple larkspur stems
- 1 pink larkspur bloom
- 4 yellow cosmos
- 4 orange cosmos
- 2 cream zinnia stems
- 3 cream zinnia blooms

Tools:
- Computer and printer
- Scissors
- Hole punch
- Tweezers
- Small paint brush

INSTRUCTIONS

Make the Book:
1. Fold the brown paper in half. Use scissors to cut along the fold, creating two 6" x 12" pieces.
2. Fold both pieces in half, and position one inside the other with the folds together.
3. Apply antiquing paint to the edges and folds of both pieces of paper for an aged look.
4. Punch two holes near the folded edges of the papers.
5. Use a computer printer to print the names of the flowers and the letters to spell out FLOWERS for the cover on plain white paper, using large letters in different fonts. Print a smaller FLOWERS for the back cover.
6. Cut out the words and individual letters. Brush all of them with antiquing paint. Let dry.
7. Lay out each page with flowers and the printed names. Use one type of flower for each page. Apply small dabs of acid-free glue on the back of each flower, leaf, and letter and attach them to the pages.
8. Apply decoupage medium with a brush to secure the edges of the flowers. Let dry.

Seal the Pages – *Optional:*
9. Carefully apply decoupage medium to cover each flower and leaf. Allow to dry completely.
10. Spray with sealer. Allow to dry.

Assemble:
11. Thread a piece of twine through the holes and knot the twine on the outside edge.
12. Thread the beads on the twine, using the photo as a guide, and knot and trim the twine. Tie knots in the ends of the twine to hold the beads in place. ❑

> **Designer's Tip:** If you will be using your flower book frequently or want to preserve your flowers for a long time, you may want to take the time to use water-diluted glue to secure the edges of the pressed flowers and seal the flowers with decoupage medium (or another sealer). I didn't seal the flowers in my book – I like the natural look and I plan to use it for display for just this year.

HEART LEAF GREETING CARD

Finding just the right leaf or flower for your cards is so much fun. A heart-shaped leaf was the inspiration for this rustic card. Mulberry paper, corrugated paper, and buttons and twine are layered with images and messages of affection.

SUPPLIES

Papers & Flowers:

- Card, 4" x 6"
- Brown mulberry paper
- Corrugated paper
- Small "love" image
- Sticker – "I love you with all my heart"
- 2 buttons
- 1 pressed leaf

Tools & Other Supplies:

- Antiquing paint
- Twine
- Scissors
- Acid-free glue
- Acid-free adhesive tape
- Small paint brush
- *Optional:* Spray sealer

INSTRUCTIONS

1. Tear the brown mulberry paper so that it is slightly smaller than the card. Use acid-free adhesive tape to attach it to the front of the card.
2. Trim the corrugated paper slightly smaller than the mulberry paper. Use the adhesive tape to attach it on top of the mulberry paper.
3. Apply antiquing paint to the edges of the card and corrugated paper. Let dry.
4. Attach the "I love you with all my heart" sticker to a piece of mulberry paper. Tear the mulberry paper around the sticker. Glue the paper with the sticker to the bottom of the corrugated paper.
5. Apply antiquing paint to the edges of the stickers and paper. Let dry.
6. Thread a 4" piece of twine through each of two buttons and tie knots in the tops. Trim the twine to desired lengths.
7. Glue the buttons to the card, using the photo as a guide.
8. Apply antiquing paint to the twine.
9. Glue the leaf to the corrugated paper.
10. Glue the "love" image at the center of the leaf.
11. *Optional:* Spray the card front with sealer, following the sealer manufacturer's instructions. Allow to dry completely. ❑

Designer's Tip: When attaching flat images to papers, I like to use acid-free adhesive tapes. But I prefer using acid-free glue when the elements are not completely flat, such as leaves and flowers.

VINTAGE GREETING

Make your greeting cards more personal and special by using your own pressed flowers and leaves to decorate them. Layer papers, buttons, and small tokens with special meaning on a card – the recipient will feel honored and loved, knowing you took time to create something just for them. Here a vintage postcard was layered on top of the greeting card piece.

SUPPLIES

Papers & Flowers:

- Blank Card, 4" x 6"
- Decorative papers
- Small postcard image
- Small "love" image
- 1 metal button
- 1 zinnia bloom or daisy
- 1 zinnia stem or daisy stem
- 1 bridal veil stem
- 1 water aven stem
- Decoupage medium

Tools & Other Supplies:

- Antiquing paint
- Tweezers
- Scissors
- Craft glue
- Acid-free adhesive tape
- Metal glue
- Small paint brush
- Disposable bowl
- *Optional:* Spray sealer

INSTRUCTIONS

1. Trim a piece of decorative paper the same size as the card. Use acid-free adhesive tape to attach it to the front of the card.
2. Use acid-free adhesive tape to attach the postcard image and the "love" image to the card, using the photo as a guide for placement.
3. Apply antiquing paint to the edges of the card, decorative paper, and images.
4. Use tweezers to position the zinnias, water aven, and bridal veil stem to the card around the postcard image.
5. Mix one part craft glue with two parts water in the disposable bowl. Remove each flower individually, apply the water-and-glue mixture to the backs with the paint brush, and replace them on the card. Allow the glue to dry.
6. Carefully cover the flowers with decoupage medium. Allow to dry completely.
7. *Optional:* Spray the card front with sealer, following the sealer manufacturer's instructions. Allow to dry completely.
8. Use the metal glue to attach the button to the postcard near the bottom. ❑

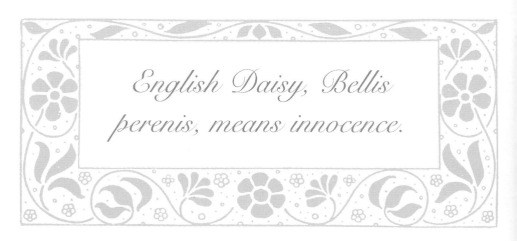

English Daisy, Bellis perenis, means innocence.

FOREVER LOVE

SCRAPBOOK PAGE

Brighten up your scrapbook pages by using complementary colors of pressed flowers to bring out the colors in your photos. You can also match images of flowers with similar colors of pressed flowers to create beautiful memory pages and displays.

SUPPLIES

Page & Floral Supplies:
- Black foam paper sheet, 12" x 12"
- 4 photos
- 2 cedar stems
- 3 basket-of-gold stems
- 1 dark blue delphinium
- 1 light blue delphinium
- 2 small brown oak leaves

Tools & Other Supplies:
- Craft glue
- Acid-free adhesive tape
- Decoupage gel
- Tweezers
- Small paint brush
- Computer printer
- Brown paper
- Disposable bowl

INSTRUCTIONS

1. Use tweezers to position the basket-of-gold on the bottom left side and the delphinium on the bottom right side of the page.
2. Mix one part craft glue with two parts water in the disposable bowl. Remove each flower, use the paint brush to apply the water-and-glue mixture to the backs, and replace them. Allow the glue to dry completely.
3. Print captions for each photo on brown paper, using a computer.
4. Arrange the photos on the page along with the printed captions. Secure the photos and captions to the paper using acid-free adhesive tape.
5. Trim the cedar stems so the cedar will lie flat against the page. Secure them to the top left, bottom right, and right side of the page with craft glue.
6. Glue the two oak leaves at bottom center.
7. Carefully cover the flowers, leaves, and cedar with decoupage gel. Allow the gel to dry completely. ❏

Mt. Rainier

Dennis, Mandi and Django

Kenon and JoyAnn

LEAF ORNAMENT

An ornament is a great holiday gift, especially when you personalize it with your own pressed flowers and leaves. Use glass ornaments, gold, silver or copper leafing and a ribbon hanger to make each one a unique design for each person. The dried materials need to be small enough to fit into the open top of the ornament. You may be able to find clear plastic ornaments that come in two parts. This will make it easier for you to get the dried materials into the ornaments.

SUPPLIES

Base & Florals:
• Glass ornament with hanger top, 4"
• 1 fall color maple leaf
• Green reindeer moss

Tools & Other Supplies:
• 12" gold metallic ribbon, 1/2" wide
• Gold leafing
• Craft glue
• Decoupage medium
• Small paint brush
• Scissors
• Spray sealer

INSTRUCTIONS

1. Remove the hanger and set aside. Fill the inside of ornament with small pieces of green reindeer moss.
2. Apply glue to the back of the maple leaf and attach it to the outside surface of the ornament. Allow the glue to dry completely.
3. Apply small amounts of glue to the ornament around the leaf and on top of the leaf. Let the glue set up slightly. Press small pieces of gold leafing on top of the glue and lightly rub across it with clean fingers. Allow the glue to dry completely.
4. Lightly brush away any excess leafing. Carefully cover the maple leaf and leafing with decoupage medium. Allow to dry.
5. Following the spray manufacturer's instructions, lightly spray the ornament with sealer. Allow to dry.
6. Replace the ornament top. Thread the gold ribbon through the hanger and knot the ribbon. Trim the ends in inverted V-shapes. ❑

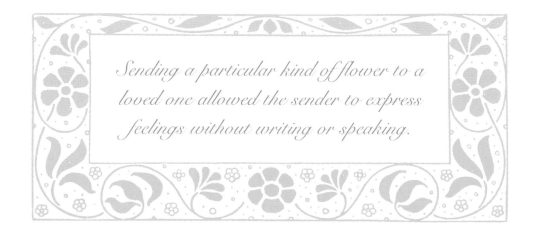

Sending a particular kind of flower to a loved one allowed the sender to express feelings without writing or speaking.

FLOWER ORNAMENT

A handmade ornament is a treasure. Gardener friends would especially like to receive them as gifts. When you visit a friend's garden, secretly pinch off some blooms from the garden plants. At Christmas, present your friend with an ornament that displays blooms from his/her own garden.

SUPPLIES

Base & Florals:

• Glass ornament with hanger, 4"

• 1 viola

• 1 water aven

• 1 bridal veil stem

Tools & Other Supplies:

• 12" gold metallic ribbon, 1/2" wide

• Gold leafing

• Tweezers

• Craft glue

• Decoupage medium

• Spray sealer

• Small paint brush

• Scissors

INSTRUCTIONS

1. Apply glue to the backs of the viola, water aven, and bridal veil. Press them to the outside surface of the ornament. Allow the glue to dry completely.

2. Apply small amounts of glue to the ornament around the flowers. Let the glue set up slightly. Press small pieces of gold leafing on top of the glue and lightly rub across it with clean fingers. Allow the glue to dry completely.

3. Lightly brush away any excess leafing. Carefully cover the flowers and leafing with decoupage medium. Allow to dry.

4. Following the sealer manufacturer's directions, lightly spray the ornaments with sealer. Allow to dry.

5. Thread gold ribbon through the ornament hanger and knot the ribbon. Trim the ribbon ends in inverted V-shapes. ❏

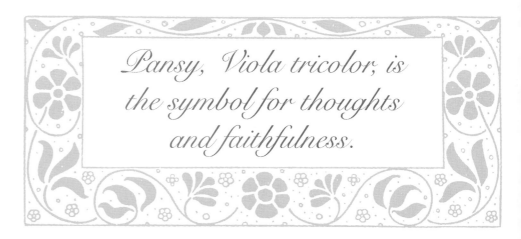

Pansy, Viola tricolor, is the symbol for thoughts and faithfulness.

DECORATED FRAMES

Also pictured on page 114

Arranging pressed flowers and leaves on frames adds interest and color, and you need only three or four blooms and a few leaves for each one. I've decorated a pair of frames, one for a rectangular print, another for an oval one, to illustrate the concept. The frames I used were decorated with painted leaves and flowers, and I arranged the dried materials to complement the painted designs.

SUPPLIES

Frames:

- 2 white painted frames with painted flowers, 8-1/4" x 10-1/4"
- 2 flower prints to fit frames

Pressed Flowers & Greenery:

- 3 coral bell stems
- 2 rue leaves
- 1 light blue delphinium
- 2 dark blue delphiniums
- 1 bridal veil stem
- 2 pink larkspur stems
- 2 maidenhair fern fronds

Tools & Other Supplies:

- Craft glue
- Spray sealer
- Decoupage medium
- Tweezers
- Small paint brush
- Disposable plastic bowl

INSTRUCTIONS

1. Use tweezers to position pressed flowers and leaves over the painted designs on the frames.
2. Mix one part craft glue with two parts water in the disposable bowl. Working one piece at a time, remove each leaf and flower and use the paint brush to apply the glue and water mixture to the back and replace on the frame. Allow the glue to dry completely.
3. Carefully cover the flowers and leaves with decoupage gel. Allow to dry completely.
4. Remove the prints and glass from the frames. Spray the frames with sealer, following the sealer manufacturer's instructions. Let dry.
5. Replace the prints and the glass. ❏

Designer's Tip: For best results, use flowers that complement the colors in the print or photo you're framing as well as the colors on the frame.

Decorated Frames

Instructions appear on page 112

TAG ART

Pictured on page 117

Add a personal touch to your gifts with individually created tags. Cover pressed leaves with gold, silver, or copper leafing or use your own pressed flowers. Personalize with the recipient's name or favorite sayings.

These little tags would also be beautiful framed. Make a tag for every flower in your garden and frame them in groups of matching frames. Three tags placed in a row in a rectangular frame is an attractive arrangement. In winter it's a nice way to remember and anticipate the growing season to come.

Ivy Leaf Tag

SUPPLIES

- Tag, 2-1/4" x 4-1/2"
- Small Tags – Good luck, clover image
- Green mulberry paper
- Postcard image
- Ivy leaf
- Gold leafing pen
- Raffia
- Antiquing paint
- Scissors
- Tweezers
- Craft glue
- Decoupage medium
- Spray sealer
- Small paint brush

INSTRUCTIONS

1. Tear the green mulberry paper so that it is slightly larger than a tag. Glue it to the tag.

2. Apply antiquing paint to the postcard image and glue it to the mulberry paper.

3. Paint the pressed ivy leaf with the gold leafing pen. Glue it to the postcard.

4. Tie a small "good luck" tag and a clover tag to the larger tag with two pieces of raffia. Trim the raffia ends.

5. Apply antiquing paint and gold leafing to the edges of the small tags, the mulberry paper, and the raffia.

6. Carefully cover the leaves and papers with decoupage medium. Allow to dry completely.

7. Following the manufacturer's instructions, spray with sealer. Allow to dry completely. ❑

TAG ART

Continued from page 115

Hydrangea Tag

SUPPLIES

- Blue tag, 2-1/4" x 4-1/2"
- Small tag – "love"
- 12 hydrangea petals
- Twine
- Scissors
- Tweezers
- Craft glue
- Decoupage medium
- Spray sealer
- Small paint brush
- Disposable bowl

INSTRUCTIONS

1. Mix one part craft glue with two parts water in the disposable bowl. Apply the water-and-glue mixture to the backs of the hydrangea petals and attach them to the tag.
2. Tie a small "love" tag to the blue tag with a piece of twine. Trim the twine ends.
3. Carefully cover the papers and flowers with decoupage medium. Allow to dry completely.
4. Following the manufacturer's instructions, spray with sealer. Allow to dry completely. ❏

Pansy Tag

SUPPLIES

- Tag, 2-1/4" x 4-1/2"
- Yellow and red decorative paper
- Postcard image with "My dear friend"
- 1 pansy
- 2 geranium leaves
- Yellow yarn
- Scissors
- Tweezers
- Craft glue
- Decoupage medium
- Spray sealer
- Small paint brush
- Hole punch
- Disposable bowl

INSTRUCTIONS

1. Trim a piece of the yellow and red decorative paper the same size as the tag. Glue it to the tag. Allow to dry.
2. Mix one part craft glue with two parts water in the disposable bowl. Use tweezers to position the geranium leaves and pansy on the paper-covered tag. Working one piece at a time, remove the leaves and pansy, apply the glue-and-water mixture to the back, and replace on the tag.
3. Trim the handwritten saying "my dear friend" from the postcard image. Punch a hole in the left side.
4. Tie the small handwritten tag to the larger tag using yellow yarn. Trim the yarn ends.
5. Carefully cover the leaves and flower with decoupage medium. Allow to dry completely.
6. Following the sealer manufacturer's instructions, spray the tag. Allow to dry completely. ❏

FRAMED FERNS

Ferns are beautiful when pressed and framed. And they press so nicely. Here, I placed several varieties between glass pieces in small contemporary frames. Use individual frames and arrange them, or use smaller attached frames for a vertical display.

SUPPLIES

Frame:

• Triple glass frame with beads, 6-1/2" square

Ferns:

• 1 mountain fern
• 2 maidenhair ferns
• 2 fan ferns

Tools & Other Supplies:

• Tweezers
• Craft glue
• Glass cleaner and paper towels
• Lint-free cloth
• Masking tape

INSTRUCTIONS

1. Remove the glass pieces from the frames. Clean them and rub with the lint-free cloth.
2. Use tweezers to position the three types of ferns on three separate pieces of glass. Working one at a time, remove each fern, apply a small dab of craft glue to the back, and replace on the glass. Allow the glue to dry.
3. Place the other piece of glass on top of the glass piece with the fern(s). Place them in the frames.
4. Place masking tape around the openings on the backs of the frames to keep the glass pieces in place. ❑

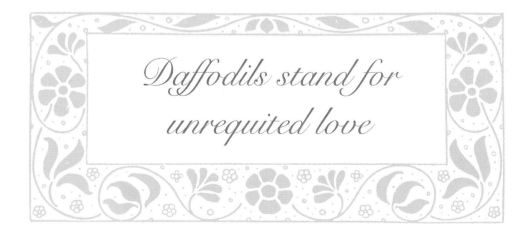

Daffodils stand for unrequited love

PHOTO ALBUM

Enjoy your favorite photos in an album that is uniquely yours. Use layers of papers, postcards, pressed flowers, and photos as mementos of special events and travels. Press flowers from your garden or bring some from your trip to make a personalized gift album for your traveling companions.

SUPPLIES

Base & Papers:

- Photo album, 8" x 9"
- Decorative papers
- Postcards or photos
- Typewriter key letters to spell the name of your destination

Pressed Flowers:

- 2 larkspur stems
- 2 wild larkspur blooms
- 1 blue delphinium bloom

Tools & Other Supplies:

- Antiquing paint
- Scissors
- Tweezers
- Craft glue
- Acid-free adhesive tape
- Decoupage medium
- Spray sealer
- Small paint brush
- Disposable bowl
- Metal glue

INSTRUCTIONS

Layer the Papers:

1. Tear the edges of a piece of decorative paper to fit the photo album cover. Brush the edges with antiquing paint. Let dry.
2. Use acid-free adhesive tape to attach the paper to the front of the album.
3. Use acid-free adhesive tape to attach postcards, stamp cutouts, and other small images to the paper on the album cover.
4. Tear a rectangular strip of paper to fit across the bottom of the album. Apply antiquing paint to the edges. Let dry.
5. Use adhesive tape to attach the paper strip to the bottom of the cover.
6. Glue the typewriter key letters on top of the paper strip using metal glue.

Add the Flowers:

7. In the disposable bowl, mix two parts water with one part craft glue.
8. Use tweezers to position the pressed flowers, using the photo as a guide. Working one pressed flower at a time, remove each one, apply the glue-and-water mixture to the back, and replace. Allow to dry.

Finish:

9. Carefully cover the flowers and papers with decoupage medium. Allow to dry.
10. Apply antiquing paint to the edges of the album cover. Allow to dry.
11. Following the sealer manufacturer's instructions, spray the album cover with sealer. Allow to dry completely. ❑

FRANCE

PHOTOGRAPHS

GLASS COASTERS

Use your favorite pressed flowers and leaves to make customized coasters for your home or for gifts. I've presented three ideas – no doubt you'll come up with many more.

You can find pre-cut glass pieces for making coasters and adhesive-backed metal tape at craft stores. CAUTION: Be very careful when handling the glass pieces – the edges are sharp.

SUPPLIES

Coaster Supplies:
- 3 glass coaster backs, 4" square
- 3 beveled glass coaster tops, 4" square
- 5 ft. adhesive-backed copper tape, 1/2" wide
- 12 clear plastic "feet"

Pressed Flowers & Leaves:
- 1 pansy
- 2 geranium leaves
- 4 fall color maple leaves
- 3 hydrangea petals

Tools & Other Supplies:
- Tweezers
- Craft glue
- Two binder clips, 1/2"
- Bone folder
- Lint-free cloth
- Glass cleaner and paper towels

INSTRUCTIONS

1. Clean the glass pieces and wipe with a lint-free cloth.
2. Place the coaster backs right side up on your work surface. Use tweezers to position the pressed flowers and leaves on the coaster backs:
   Pansy coaster: Geranium leaves with a pansy on top
   Maple leaf coaster: Maple leaves
   Hydrangea coaster: Hydrangea petals
   Use the photo as a guide for placement. After arranging, working one piece at a time, remove each flower and leaf, apply glue to the back, and replace. Allow the glue to dry completely.
3. Place the flat side of one beveled coaster top on one coaster back. Put small pieces of paper towel on opposite sides of the two glass pieces and carefully place binder clips over the paper towel pieces to hold the glass pieces together. Check the positioning of the glass pieces and be sure the edges are even.
4. Cut 18" of copper tape. Peel the backing from 1" of the copper tape and press it against one edge of the coaster. Continue wrapping the coaster with the tape, removing the alligator clips and paper towel pieces as needed. Press the tape against the edges on all four sides, then press the edges against the front and back. Fold the corners at angles (like wrapping a package).
5. Smooth the tape, using a bone folder.
6. Attach the four plastic feet to the bottom.
7. Repeat steps 3 through 6 to complete the remaining two coasters. ❑

Supplies for Making Coasters, pictured left to right: Adhesive-backed metal tape, tweezers, beveled glass top pieces, flat glass coaster backs, plastic "feet," binder clips

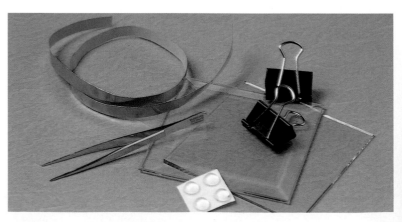

FRAMED HYDRANGEA

This idea can be used to create framed reminders of all of your favorite flowers after you press them. Here, I've re-created a beautiful hydrangea bloom from fragile tiny pressed petals by layering petals in different shades of lavender, pink, blue, and green. I used a real hydrangea stem, flattened with a hammer, and pressed my own hydrangea leaves.

SUPPLIES

Frame & Background:

- Barn wood frame with glass, 13" x 11"
- Decorative paper, 12" x 12" (for the background)

Plant Materials:

- 35 pink and blue hydrangea petal groups
- 4 hydrangea leaves
- 1 hydrangea stem, 7"

Tools & Other Supplies:

- Scissors
- Tweezers
- Hammer
- Acid-free glue
- Pencil

INSTRUCTIONS

1. Remove the backing and glass from the frame. Position the glass on the decorative paper and use the pencil to trace around the glass.
2. Cut out the paper, using scissors. If needed, clean the glass.
3. Using a hammer, flatten the hydrangea stem.
4. Use tweezers to position the hydrangea petals, stem, and leaves on the paper, using the photo as a guide for placement.
5. Place the frame over the paper to check the placement of the petals, stem, and leaves. Adjust, if needed, being sure the plant materials are visible with the frame in place.
6. Remove the stem and leaves. Put dots of glue on the backs and position on the paper.
7. Individually remove each petal group and place a small dot of glue on the back of each one. Re-position on the paper. Allow the glue to dry completely.
8. Replace the glass. Install the paper with the leaves and flowers in the frame. Replace the frame backing. ❏

Flower language allowed intentions to be declared, refusals and acceptances to be made, assignations arranged and lovers dismissed.

METRIC CONVERSION CHART

Inches to Millimeters and Centimeters

Inches	MM	CM	Inches	MM	CM
1/8	3	.3	2	51	5.1
1/4	6	.6	3	76	7.6
3/8	10	1.0	4	102	10.2
1/2	13	1.3	5	127	12.7
5/8	16	1.6	6	152	15.2
3/4	19	1.9	7	178	17.8
7/8	22	2.2	8	203	20.3
1	25	2.5	9	229	22.9
1-1/4	32	3.2	10	254	25.4
1-1/2	38	3.8	11	279	27.9
1-3/4	44	4.4	12	305	30.5

Yards to Meters

Yards	Meters	Yards	Meters
1/8	.11	3	2.74
1/4	.23	4	3.66
3/8	.34	5	4.57
1/2	.46	6	5.49
5/8	.57	7	6.40
3/4	.69	8	7.32
7/8	.80	9	8.23
1	.91	10	9.14
2	1.83		

INDEX

INDEX